Collins Revision

KS3

English

Revision Guide

Levels 3–5

Kim Richardson

Revision Guide Contents

Workbook Contents

About Key Stage 3 English

This book has been written to help you practise the necessary skills to raise your level in Key Stage 3 English. It gives you lots of practice texts to analyse, different types of questions to try and helpful tips and hints on how to improve. It will give you the confidence to make good progress at KS3 and then GCSE.

What does Key Stage 3 English involve?

- KS3 English is split into three skill areas: reading, writing and speaking and listening (speaking and listening is counted as one).

Reading

- You will have lessons and assessments that focus on your analytical skills. This means you have to consider how the text is written, why it is written and the impact it has on the reader.

- There are lots of activities and support in this book to help you develop your reading skills.

Writing

- During KS3 English you will also spend lots of time planning and writing different sorts of material. The work you do on improving your reading skills will help you understand how to write effectively and get higher marks.

- Your written work will cover lots of different purposes such as writing to argue, describe and even review.

- Once again, we've included plenty of activities to support you as you learn to develop these skills.

Speaking and listening

- Don't forget this really important part of English! As you learn about Reading and Writing you'll also develop your Speaking and Listening skills – essential to communicate well in all situations.

- Try explaining your ideas about the activities and texts in this book to someone – this is a great way to develop your confidence get your message across effectively.

And finally... literature

- As well as English, you'll also study Literature at school, often in the same lesson. Reading poetry, prose and plays is a great way to develop your key English skills.

- You'll study various authors, from pre-1914 to modern day, but the most famous one has to be Shakespeare!

- You have to study at least one of Shakespeare's plays in Key Stage 3 and another in Key Stage 4, so it's good to get as much practice as possible now. This book contains all you need to impress your teacher and classmates as you start to study one of the greatest English playwrights.

Top Tip!

The more you read, the more your English skills will improve.

Different text types

- Throughout your Key Stage 3 course, you will read a variety of texts and will be assessed on how you evaluate the pieces of writing and how you answer questions on them.

- Your teacher may give you different texts to compare, sometimes on the same **topic** (e.g. animals), but they will be written in very different **styles**.

- They will normally include fiction and non-fiction texts. The non-fiction texts will be in different **forms**, e.g. book extract, newspaper report, interview, leaflet … all sorts.

- The texts will have different **purposes**, e.g. to explain, to tell a story, to persuade an audience, to review a film.

Pages 8, 12, 16, 20, 24 (different types of text).

How to read a text

- When you are practising your comprehension skills, make sure you take your time to read the extract carefully.

- As you read, you can highlight or underline any **key words or phrases**. Also, try to notice **key features** of the texts, such as their structure, how language is used and the mood or tone of the writing.

Pages 10, 14, 18, 22, 26 (key features).

- You don't need to remember everything in the texts. You will be able to re-read the important bits when you answer the questions.

Different question types

- In practice tests, some questions may be short, and only give you 1 mark each. Others will be longer, and may give you up to 5 marks.

- You may be asked to write a word, a sentence or a paragraph. You may be asked to tick a box, fill in a table or complete a sentence.

- The questions may ask you to:
  - **find information**
  - **comment** on language or structure
  - give your **opinion**
  - **explain** the writer's **viewpoint and purpose**.

Pages 28–37 (answering different types of question).

Answering the questions

- Start at the beginning and work your way through the questions in order. The first few questions refer to the first text in the reading booklet, and so on.

- **Do exactly what you are asked.** For example, if you are asked to write a word or phrase, don't write an essay.

- Look at the **marks** given for each question. They will give you an idea about how much you should write.

Top Tip!

You will be assessed on:
- whether you answer the **precise** question ✓
- how well you understand and can comment on the texts ✓

You will *not* be assessed on:
- your writing style ✗
- your spelling, punctuation or grammar ✗

Good practice

- When doing practice tests, use the **marks** as a guide. You shouldn't spend more than 2 minutes per mark.

- Leave 5 minutes at the end to **read through and check** your answers.

Spot Check

Look at these questions. What type of answer is each question asking for? **a** giving your opinion, **b** finding information, **c** commenting on language.

1 Which words show that Sam is frightened?

2 Comment on the writer's use of language to describe how frightened Sam is.

3 What do you think Sam is most frightened of in this passage?

What is fiction?

- Fiction means **stories**. Common forms are short stories and novels (longer stories).

- Fiction describes imaginary events in a way that entertains the reader.

- The key features of a story to comment on are the **plot**, **language**, **setting** and **characters**.

Pages 10–11 (characters).

Plot

- The plot is the **storyline**. Plots often have an introduction, a development (build up), a crisis (when the story comes to a head) and a resolution (when things are sorted out).

- **Fast moving** plots are exciting and full of tension. **Slow moving** plots focus more on character, mood and description.

Language

- Words are chosen carefully to create a precise effect. Writers use **descriptive detail** and draw vivid pictures (**imagery**) as in this extract from the text opposite: *for a moment the page of the London A to Z he was supposed to be reading blurred and swam beneath his eyes.*

- Writers pay attention to the **structure** of their sentences. Notice the length of these sentences: *Quickly he knuckled the wet from his face. Had his mother noticed? If she had, he would say it was sweat. And that he felt sick.*

Setting

- The setting is the **place** and **time** in which the story is set.

- The way the author describes the setting contributes to the **mood** or **atmosphere** of the story. The extract opposite is set in a hot, smelly meat market. It helps to create a stifling, heavy atmosphere.

Spot Check

1 What are the four key features of stories?
2 Explain what the resolution of a story is.
3 Think about a novel or short story you have read. What is the plot?

Question

This is the opening passage from a novel.

List two things which are intended to grab the reader's interest.

> It was the stench seeping in through the car windows that bothered Tom the most. Rank and beefy, it reminded him of the way dogs smell after a walk in the rain. Smelly dogs made him think of Goldie, left behind in Dorset, and for a moment the page of the London *A to Z* he was supposed to be reading blurred and swam beneath his eyes.
>
> Quickly he knuckled the wet from his face. Had his mother noticed? If she had, he would say it was sweat. And that he felt sick. It was late morning, the middle of August, and hot enough for even a skinny twelve year old to be melting like a lolly. Add the stink of Smithfield meat market, leaching through traffic fumes, and anyone with nostrils and a stomach in working order was bound to feel bad.

(From *Follow Me Down*, by Julie Hearn)

Answer

1 The good description of the smell draws us in to the story. The author uses vivid and powerful language, for example the words 'stench' and 'rank and beefy', to make us feel we are really there.

2 The author implies that the boy is in London, but we want to know what he is doing there and why he has left his dog behind.

Top Tip!

To get a level 5 you need to be able to comment on how the writer **implies** (not just states) what is going on. That means reading between the lines.

Did YOU Know?

The author John Creasey wrote 565 books in 40 years. Twenty-six of them were written in a single year!

Characters

- **Believable** and **interesting** characters are central to the success of a story.

- Things happen to characters, but characters also **develop** (change) through a story.

- Characters affect each other. These **relationships** are often the key aspects of a story.

Describing characters

You can learn about characters in different ways:

- by **how they look**, e.g. *He had small piercing eyes that were set too closely together.*

- by **how they speak**, e.g. *"Found a shilling, huh?" His voice was gruff. "Want to show me?"*

- by **what they do**, e.g. *He sidled up to me, then grabbed at my hand and sank his teeth into it.*

> **Top Tip!**
> To get a level 5 you need to be able to show that you understand what a character is **feeling**, not just what he or she is like.

Dialogue

- Characters' speech is called **dialogue**.

- Dialogue can include different **accents** (pronunciation) and **dialect** (e.g. regional versions of speech).

- Each character will have their own way of speaking, which will be **consistent** through the story.

Narrative viewpoint

- The point of view from which the story is told is called the **narrative viewpoint**.

- A **1st person narrative** is written as if one of the characters is telling it, e.g. *I opened the package carefully.*

- A **3rd person narrative** is told by the author, e.g. *Nasreem opened the package carefully.*

Read the extract on page 9 again.

What do we learn about the character Tom?

Answer

Tom is in a car. We know that because of the car windows in the first sentence. He's also in London, though he comes from Dorset, where his dog has been left behind – 'left behind in Dorset'.

We also learn that it is very smelly. This is because of the meat market, which they must be driving through or near. It makes him feel really bad. In fact it 'bothered Tom the most'.

Tom is also very hot, it is August. He's twelve years old and skinny.

level 5

Comment

This is a level 5 answer because it covers the main points that we are told about Tom. It also shows some understanding of Tom, including his feeling of being bothered by the smell. This point is backed up by a relevant quotation from the text.

The answer would gain a higher level if it mentioned Tom's sadness (rather than focusing on the dog), as well as his attempt to hide his feelings from his mother. More detailed and relevant reference to the text would also add marks.

Did You Know?

The evil Professor Snape in the Harry Potter books is supposed to be based on the head of science who taught the author, J K Rowling.

**pot Check**

1 What is a 1st person narrative?
2 Name three ways in which an author can show what a character is like.
3 What is the difference between accent and dialect?

Purpose and audience

Some texts try to get the reader to do something, e.g. buy a product or agree with the writer's point of view. For example:

- Adverts may try to **persuade** you to buy an iPod.

- Newspaper articles may **argue** that footballers get paid too much.

- Health leaflets and magazine articles may **advise** you on how to eat properly.

> **Top Tip!**
>
> When commenting on an extract, remember to think about why it has been written. Point out how the words and layout suit the writer's **purpose**.

Structure

- The writing is usually presented as a series of points in a **logical order**.

- The **first sentence** in a paragraph or advert often makes the main point.

- Particular **words and phrases** are used to show how the points are connected or developed, e.g. *however, another point is …, in addition, on the other hand*.

- There is usually a powerful **opening** and **ending**.

Rhetorical techniques

Rhetorical techniques help get the message across effectively. Here are some examples:

- **Repetition**, e.g. *Let there be justice for all. Let there be peace for all.*

- Using 'you' to address the audience directly, and 'we' to include the audience on the writer's side.

- **Sound effects**, e.g. alliteration (*nuisance neighbours*) and rhyme (*a bad law, not a mad law*).

- **Emotive language** – language designed to make the audience feel something strongly, e.g. *They are destroying children's lives.*

Design and layout

Adverts and leaflets need to be **attractive** and **easy to read**. They may include:

- **Pictures** In an advert the picture may be very important.

- **Columns** The text is often in columns to make it easy to read.

- **Design** Colour, font style and size, use of bold/italic, graphics – all help to get the message across.

- **Subheadings** They break up the text into sections and guide the reader.

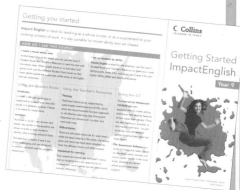

Example

Look at this example of a typical advice text:

Understanding the reader's problems/fears

Question to draw reader in

Worried about getting spots? The best thing is to eat a healthy balanced diet. It's not too difficult – you just need to:
- *have at least 5 portions of fruit and veg every day*
- *eat starchy foods, such as potatoes and rice*
- *go easy on the dairy products, such as cheese and milk.*

Addresses reader directly

Verbs tell reader what to do

Bullet point list to make points easy to follow

Conversational (informal) tone

Did You Know?

The first advert on TV was for Gibbs toothpaste, in 1955. The slogan was, "It's tingling fresh. It's fresh as ice. It's Gibbs SR toothpaste."

Spot Check

1 What is the purpose of an advert?
2 Give two ways in which adverts achieve their purpose.
3 Why do texts that persuade, argue or advise often begin with a question?

Fact

A **fact** is something that **can be proved** to be true:

- *Peter Jackson's film 'King Kong' was made in 2005.*

- *Wayne Rooney is a footballer.*

If people don't agree, you can check facts and show them the evidence.

Opinion

An **opinion** is someone's **point of view**:

- *'King Kong' was a fabulous film.*

- *Rooney's shot was unstoppable.*

These opinions cannot be proved to be true. They are the beliefs or judgements of the writer.

Where you find opinions

Opinions are found in all sorts of writing, e.g.

- **reviews** – where the reviewer gives their opinion about a film, CD or book

- **adverts** – where the audience is persuaded to agree with an opinion about a product

- **newspaper** and **magazine articles**, which argue for or against an opinion.

Persuasive opinions

Opinions can be very persuasive, so that you believe they are true:

- They can **disguise themselves as facts**, e.g. *Everyone knows that ...*

- They can use **powerful words**, especially adjectives, e.g. *a perfect gift for Christmas* or *an appalling waste of money.*

- They can use **emotive language** e.g. *the holiday of your dreams* or *These men are preying on our children.*

Read this extract from a Greenpeace advert.

Give three examples of how the writer uses fact and opinion to persuade the reader to help the campaign.

fact – '80% of the world's ancient forests'. 80% is a lot.

opinion – LOVE. This word and the picture make you want to preserve the orang-utan.

Protecting ancient forests

A staggering 80% of the world's ancient forests have already been destroyed or degraded. Each year, millions of hectares of ancient forests are logged, often illegally, driven by international demand for cheap timber and other wood products, including paper. The UK is Europe's worst offender, with up to 50% of our tropical plywood coming from Indonesia's pristine rainforests. In Indonesia, an estimated 80% of the orang-utan's natural habitats have been wiped out in the last 20 years.

LOVE

opinion – 'The UK is Europe's worst offender'. It makes you want to stop your own country destroying forests.

Top Tip!

- To gain average marks you must **show the techniques** a writer has used to persuade the audience.
- To gain top marks you need to **explain how the writer has used** those techniques.

Did You Know?

It has been estimated that there are over a million words in the English language – over two million if all scientific terms are included.

pot Check

1 Are these facts or opinions?
   a It makes no difference if you skip breakfast.
   b Some people eat eggs and bacon for breakfast.
2 What is the effect of the emotive language used in this headline:

BUNNIES SLAUGHTERED IN THEIR THOUSANDS FOR FUR COATS

Reading texts that inform and recount

INFORMATION

Look out for these key features:

Purpose and audience

- **Information** texts include reference books, travel guides and leaflets.

- Their **purpose** is to give information about people, places and things.

- You read them to find out about something.

Structure

- Clear **organisation** and **logical order** of topics. **Subheadings** guide reader.

- **General statements** or **main points** first, then examples.

- **Tables** and **diagrams** might add information.

Language

- **Present tense** and **3rd person** (*he, she, it*) used.

- Clear, concise sentences.

- Usually **formal** English, and can include specialist words.

Top Tip!

If you are asked to comment on the layout of an information leaflet, think about the images, colours, font style and size, as well as how the images and writing work together.

RECOUNT

Look out for these key features:

Purpose and audience

- **Recount** texts include newspaper reports, travel writing and biography.

- Their **purpose** is to retell events.

- You read them to find out what happened, and often to be entertained.

Structure

- Events are generally told in **time order**.

- **Time connectives** guide the reader, e.g. *then* or *the following day*.

- New **paragraphs** mark a change of focus, such as a new time, place or person.

Language

- **Past tense**, though present tense may be used in newspaper stories.

- **Descriptive language** to bring events to life.

Page 18.

- Specific **details** given – dates, times, names, descriptions.

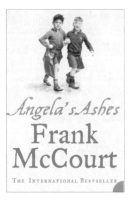

Articles in popular newspapers give information in a particular way:

Headline in full caps.

Subheading tells you more about the subject of the article.

1st paragraph sums up the article.

Next few paragraphs give **more detail**.

Each **paragraph** is only one sentence.

Subheading used to catch eye and break up text.

Photos and **layout** important in popular newspaper stories.

DEATH OF THE LADETTE
Old-fashioned girls don't want to party

■ by LAURA NEILL

BRITISH women are rejecting the ladette lifestyle for an old-fashioned family role.

They're turning their backs on the hard partying made famous by the likes of Sarah Cox, 31, and Zoe Ball, 34.

Instead the so-called 'new traditionalists' are married with children.

And they put the family before money and career, though they can combine both.

The new generation of 25 to 45-year-olds has been identified in a new survey.

They admire the values of their mother's era and believe in cooking and knitting, which has become trendy with the stars.

Twist

They snub food fads but know enough about health issues to realise what they should and shouldn't eat, according to the study for drinks firm Ovaltine.

Interviews with 500 women in the 25-45 age group found many wanted life to be 'more like the old days' with a modern twist.

Did You Know?

The book ...*All That Men Know About Women*, which was published in 1996, has 200 pages – but they're all blank!

Spot Check

1 What is a biography?
2 'Diaries and autobiographies are written in the 1st person.' True or false?
3 What tense would you expect to be used in a description of the first moon landing?

Using the senses

* The senses are: looking, hearing, smelling, tasting and feeling. A good writer will make you use your senses:

  I felt my legs buckle beneath me. The ground rose up and hit me between my eyes. The earth didn't taste too good.

* A **visual image** is particularly important, as it lets the reader 'see' what is happening.

Imagery

Look out for these special ways of creating an image, or picture:

* **similes**, which compare something to something else, e.g. *Each harsh word was like the lash of a whip.*

* **metaphors**, which describe something as something else, e.g. *His body was a finely tuned machine which needed constant maintenance.*

* **personification**, which describes non-human things as if they were people, e.g. *The wind provided a helping hand as he cycled up the final hill.*

> **Top Tip!**
>
> Remember that a **simile** uses the words 'like' or 'as' to compare two things. A **metaphor** describes something directly as another thing.

Powerful words

* **Verbs** are 'doing' words. Precise or colourful verbs are very effective in passages describing action, e.g. *The eagle plummeted* (rather than 'dived'), *He hurled the book* (rather than 'threw').

* **Adjectives** are describing words, which usually go with nouns. They can make descriptions more vivid and detailed, e.g. *The piercing noise caused a frenzied squealing in the pig pens.*

Spot Check   What kind of imagery are these?
1 On the morning of my exam the sun rose reluctantly.
2 The flames of her hair crackled as she tossed her head.
3 He used his pen like a sword to attack his critics.

Read this email, which Ellen MacArthur sent on day 21 of her record-breaking voyage round the world.

Identify two things which make her description of the storm effective.

New Message

Send New Attach Find Font Print

To:

Subject:

Last night was a dark night, hard to see anything out there – nothing but the constant noise of B&Q[1] speeding through the water, the howling wind and the breaking of the waves. The waves are so steep here that poor B&Q feels like she's either running down a hill or being pushed hard up one. Waves regularly break on the windward float quarter. What is noticeable through the dark, shining brighter than our glowing instruments, are the crests of phosphorescence[2] – unbelievable, beautiful, and at times immense. We spend our time, even when trying to rest huddled in a ball in the cuddy[3], just feeling where we are on each mountain, how fast, how far and when will we hit the bottom …

---

[1] Ellen's boat
[2] tiny sea creatures that glow in the dark
[3] small sheltered area on board

Answer

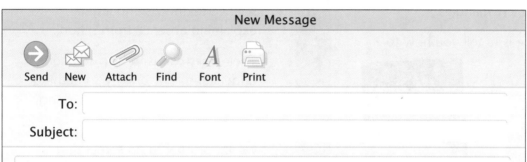

level
5

1 Ellen uses the senses. She makes us see things (the dark, then the glowing creatures) and hear things (the howling wind and breaking waves). She also tells us what she feels like in the last sentence.

2 Ellen also uses a metaphor – she describes the waves as hills, and later on as mountains.

Did You Know?

There are some unusual collective nouns in English, including an 'orchestra' of computers and a 'kindle' of kittens.

Reading texts that instruct and explain

INSTRUCTION

Look out for these key features:

Purpose and audience

- **Instruction** texts include recipes, directions and DIY manuals.

- Their **purpose** is to tell you how to do something.

- You read one to find out how to do something.

Structure

- A series of step-by-step instructions in **time order**.

- May begin with a **list** of materials/ingredients needed.

- **Layout** makes the instructions easy to follow. May include diagrams, a numbered list, etc.

Language

- Uses **present tense**, **direct address** (you...) and **commands**, e.g. *Break six eggs into a bowl.*

- Written in **simple**, **clear sentences**, in formal English. Paragraphs are short.

- Includes **time connectives** to show the order you need to follow, e.g. *first* or *then*.

EXPLANATION

Look out for these key features:

Purpose and audience

- **Explanation** texts include science textbooks and letters explaining absence from school.

- Their **purpose** is to help someone understand how or why something happens, or how to do something.

- You read one to find out how something works, or how to do something.

Structure

- A series of **logical steps**.

- Each new point has a **new paragraph**.

- **Diagrams** or **illustrations** may help explain what to do.

Language

- **Present tense** used.

- **Connectives** guide the reader, e.g. *because* or *as a result* showing that one thing causes another. Time connectives, e.g. *next*, show the order.

- **Formal language**, e.g. *An electric current is generated by special muscle cells in the fish.* **Technical terms** may be used.

Page 26 (formal language).

Top Tip!

To gain a level 5 you need to be able to say **why** a text has been written (its purpose).

Example

Note the key features of this instruction text. It is an extract from a recipe.

Clear format – a **numbered list**

1 Chop up a red cabbage and slice it thinly. Next, heat a saucepan of clean water until it boils.

2 Carefully add the cabbage to the boiling water. Then take the pan off the heat. Leave it to cool.

Time connectives

Sequence of points in chronological order. Each **paragraph** is a new point.

Direct address – note **commands**

Present tense and **short, simple sentences**

Did You Know?

The first English cookbook, 'Forme of Cury', was written in 1390 by the cooks of Richard II. These weren't curry recipes – 'cury' was the Old English word for 'cooking'!

Spot Check

1 What kind of text are the rules of the card game Racing Demon?

2 Why do instructions use direct address?

3 What kind of connectives are 'then', 'next', 'the following day'?

Putting texts together

Structure refers to the way in which a text or passage is put together. This depends on its **purpose**:

• An **instruction** text is made up of a clear sequence of steps.

• An **argument** text may begin with the key point of view, then give reasons and evidence, then conclude.

• A **narrative** text may have an introduction, a development, a crisis and a resolution.

Page 8.

What makes a good structure?

• The points are **well organised** – in time order (e.g. for instructions) or with the main points first.

• A new **paragraph** is used for each new point or topic.

• Paragraphs may begin with **the main point**, or a general point, and continue with the detail.

• **Connectives** show how the ideas are linked, and where the ideas are going, e.g. *in addition* or *next*.

From start to finish

Structure also refers to the way in which a text begins and ends:

• The **beginning** may introduce a topic, or draw the reader in with some powerful language or ideas.

• The **end** may sum up the passage (a conclusion), or have a surprising twist, or neatly refer back to the beginning in some way.

Top Tip!

If you are commenting on the **structure** of a text, ask yourself what type of text it is. The way it is structured needs to suit the **purpose** of the text.

Spot Check

1 How do connectives help the structure of a passage?
2 When would you expect to find a new paragraph in a text?
3 Name two different ways in which a passage could end.

Look again at this extract from a recipe.

Give two ways in which the writer has made the sequence of steps clear.

> 1 Chop up a red cabbage and slice it thinly. Next, heat a saucepan of clean water until it boils.
>
> 2 Carefully add the cabbage to the boiling water. Then take the pan off the heat. Leave it to cool.

Top Tip!

Try to use key words from the question in your answer. This will keep your answer really focused.

Answer

1 The writer has put numbers against each step.

2 He or she has used words like 'next' and 'then' which shows clearly the order that you do things.

Comment

This answer is simple but gains full marks. It answers the precise question. Two methods have been listed and there are quotes from the text to back up the second point.

The student uses the word 'clearly' in the answer, which shows she or he is following the question and that the answer is relevant. It's a good ploy to use!

Did You Know?

In his novel *The French Lieutenant's Woman* (1969), the author John Fowles gives the reader a choice of two endings – a happy one or a sad one.

Reading texts that discuss and review

DISCUSSION TEXTS

Look out for these key features:

Purpose and audience

- **Discussion** texts include newspaper articles on important issues and student essays.

- Their **purpose** is to analyse an issue, exploring different points of view.

- They differ from argument texts because they present a **balanced view**.

Structure

- An **introduction** states the issue to be discussed.

- Each **view**, or point, is explored in turn.

- **Connectives** help the reader through the text, e.g. *however* or *another point is …*

- A **conclusion** may summarise the arguments or give a personal view.

Language

- **Present tense** and **3rd person** (*he, she, it*), e.g. *Some evidence suggests …*

- **Formal** language and tone – the arguments are presented fairly.

REVIEWS

Look out for these key features:

Purpose and audience

- A **review** is a way of **giving an opinion** in detail about a book, CD, film, etc.

- It is meant to **inform** the reader, and **persuade** them to buy/read/watch the work (or not!).

- You read reviews to find out about the work.

Structure

- It often begins with some basic **information** about the work.

- A series of **paragraphs** covers different points, e.g. a book review may cover plot, characters, setting and style.

- A **conclusion** may sum up the reviewer's opinion.

Language

- **Present tense** with **3rd person** when describing the work, e.g. *The film is fabulous.*

- Sentences packed with **detail**, e.g. *It mixes rip-roaring action writing with high-tech funk.*

- Often a **friendly** and **informal tone** to get on the reader's side, e.g. *What a yawn of a book.*

YAWN

Top Tip!

Most discussion texts are serious – look out for **formal** language. Most reviews are lighter in tone – look out for **informal** language.

Note the features of this review of a computer game:

**Games
Imperial Glory
PC/Eidos £39.99**

Basic **information** listed at the start.

Sentences packed with **detail**.

Friendly and informal **tone**.

Step this way commander … *Imperial Glory* takes the bloodthirsty Napoleonic era (roughly) and pits the vying continental superpowers against one another in encounters reminiscent of *Rome Total War*.

Tactics play a key role as you bid to wheel your cavalry behind your foe, take an area of high ground or match your troops against the enemy's. And there's the added bonus of naval battles, though you'll probably leave the marine war to go to the sea dogs while you concentrate on hacking down the Queen's finest with your Cossacks.

IG is an accessible and satisfying strategy game on a grand scale. A valuable addition to the ranks for any PC general.

Introduction draws reader in and gives a general description of the game.

New paragraph goes into more detail about features of the game.

Conclusion is a short summary of writer's view.

Paperback books were not produced until 1935. They were an instant success, bringing books to a much wider audience.

Spot Check

1 Why should discussion texts be balanced?
2 Why might you read a CD review?
3 If a review covers plot, direction, acting and special effects, what is it reviewing?

Tone

- Tone refers to the **mood** or **style** of a piece of writing, e.g. a light-hearted tone, a serious tone or an angry tone.

- The tone a writer chooses depends on the **purpose** and **audience** of the writing. For example, an advice leaflet aimed at teenagers will have a more conversational tone than a news report in a serious newspaper.

Identifying tone

To identify the tone of a piece of writing, you need to look at **word choice**, **content** and **structure**, e.g:

- Slang terms give writing a more **conversational** tone, e.g. *in your face* or *street cred*.

- Writing in the 2nd person (*you*) is **more personal** than using the 3rd person (*he/she/it*).

- Exaggeration and jokes add a **humorous** tone.

- Long sentences and paragraphs often add a **more serious** tone.

Top Tip!

To help you identify tone, imagine you are reading the piece of writing aloud. What tone of voice would you use?

Formality

Formal language gives writing a **serious** tone. It:

- follows all the rules of English grammar

- uses more difficult or technical words, e.g. *institutions* or *population*

- uses more complex sentences, e.g. *Although he became king in October, it was not until December that …*

Informal language gives writing a **lighter** tone. It:

- includes slang or colloquialisms, e.g. *cool* or *ain't*

- includes more contractions, e.g. *isn't, can't* or *won't*

- is more personal, e.g. *You could think about …*

- uses simpler words, including 'fillers', e.g. *well* or *yes, but …*

Question

The review on page 25 has a personal tone in places.

Identify two phrases that are personal, and say why they have been used.

Answer

1 'Step this way commander' is personal because it addresses the reader directly, asking them to be the general in the game. It grabs your attention from the start.

2 'match your troops' imagines that you are already playing this game.

Comment

This answer gets full marks. The student has chosen two good examples and shown an understanding of the purpose of the writing.

Did You Know?

Standard English is the name given to the kind of English you are taught to write in schools. Hardly anyone speaks it, though, except newsreaders on the TV or radio.

7PM

pot Check

1 Which piece of advice has a more gentle tone:
   – *It is important for everyone's health that they drink eight glasses of water each day.*
   – *Can you up your water intake by drinking up to eight glasses a day?*
2 Arrange in order of formality:
   – *It's really nice.*
   – *It is perfectly delightful.*
   – *That's wicked, man.*

Finding information

The questions

Some short questions ask you to **find information** in the extract.
Often this is the first question asked about an extract.

Here are some examples (about the extract opposite):

1 How long has Ginger been sleeping rough?

2 What part of the country is Link from?

Answering the questions

• You have to **scan** the extract to look for the information you want.
  Sometimes you are told where to look, e.g. *In the first paragraph, find …*

• Give **only** the information you are asked for, e.g. (question 1):

  • Six or seven months ✓

  • Ginger has been sleeping rough for six or seven months. ✓

  • Ginger has been sleeping rough for six or seven months.
    He comes from Birmingham. ✗

• Simply copy the key word or phrase that you are asked for. Don't add
  extra information. You don't need to write in complete sentences.

Top Tip!
Don't spend too long on this type of question. They are worth only 1 or 2 marks.

Did You Know?
Rudyard Kipling, the author of *Jungle Book*, once painted his golf balls red so that he could play in the snow.

Spot Check

Look at these statements about questions that ask you to find information. Are they true or false?
1 You don't have to write complete sentences.
2 You need to know information that isn't in the extract.
3 They are worth a lot of marks.

Read this passage about Link, a teenager who finds himself homeless in London. It describes his first night in a street doorway.

I'd just wriggled into my sleeping-bag and dropped my head on my pack when he arrived. I heard these footsteps and thought, keep going. Go past. Please go past, but he didn't. The footsteps stopped and I knew he was looking down at me. I opened my eyes. He was just a shadow framed in the doorway. "This your place?" I croaked. Stupid question. He was going to say yes even if it wasn't, right? What I should have said was piss off. I wondered how big he was.

"No, you're right, mate." He sounded laid back, amiable. "Just shove up a bit so I can spread my roll." I obliged and he settled himself beside me, so close we were almost touching. It felt good to be with someone. Now, if anybody else turned up it wouldn't matter. There were two of us. I felt I ought to say something so I said, "Been doing this long?" hoping he wouldn't be offended.

"Six, seven months," he said. "You?"

"First night."

He chuckled. "I can tell. Where you from?"

"Up north."

"Brum, me."

"I can tell." It was a risk, this crack about his accent, but he only chuckled again. "Name's Ginger," he said, and waited.

(From *Stone Cold*, by Robert Swindells)

1 What was Link's reaction when he heard footsteps?

2 What reason does Link give for feeling good about sharing the doorway with someone else?

1 He wanted the person to keep going.

2 If anybody else turned up, it wouldn't matter.

READING   Understanding the text

The questions

Some questions ask you to 'read between the lines' of the passage. This means looking for things that aren't always stated clearly. You need to understand what the author is **suggesting**.

Here are some examples of questions like this (all relate to the passage on page 29):

1 Write down two words or phrases which show Link is unsure about the right things to say or do.

2 Give two reasons why Link may have wanted the footsteps to 'keep going'.

3 What impression do you get of Ginger? Refer to the text in your answer.

Answering the questions

- Sometimes you are simply asked to scan for the right **words or phrases**, e.g. (question 1):

'Stupid question', 'I felt I ought to say something'

- Sometimes you need to give a **longer answer**, e.g. (question 2):

Link may have wanted the footsteps to keep going because he was frightened of being moved on by the police. Or he may have thought he was going to be attacked.

- You may be asked to **refer to the text** in your answer. This means quoting the relevant bit and explaining what it shows, e.g. (question 3):

Ginger seems to be very laid back. He doesn't pretend that it is his place. Instead he says, 'No, you're right, mate'. He chuckles when he's talking to Link.

Top Tip!

You have to **imagine** what Link is feeling – it isn't stated directly.

Top Tip!

If the passage is a story, try to imagine what the characters are thinking or feeling. Getting 'under their skin' will help you answer this sort of question.

Spot Check

1 What does 'reading between the lines' mean?
2 'You can give your own opinion when answering this sort of question?' True or false?

We get different impressions of Link's state of mind in this passage (see page 29).

Complete the table by writing down two more quotations from the extract and explaining what each of them suggests about Link's state of mind.

Quotation	What this suggests about Link's state of mind
"This your place?" I croaked.	He is worried that he has taken someone else's sleeping place.

Answer

Quotation	What this suggests about Link's state of mind
"This your place?" I croaked.	He is worried that he has taken someone else's sleeping place.
I wondered how big he was.	Link was anxious in case he was going to be attacked.
I felt I ought to say something.	He is nervous about leaving a silence between them.

Comment

This answer gets full marks because it gives two suitable quotations and describes what each quotation suggests about Link's state of mind. There are several other quotations that could have been used instead, e.g. *'It felt good to be with someone'* (He is relieved not to be alone.)

Did You Know?

Bruno Hauptmann kidnapped and murdered a baby, and was sent to the electric chair in 1936. What gave him away was his habit of adding extra 'e's to the end of words. He did this in his ransom note.

The questions

Some questions ask you to comment on the way a writer **organises** the text. This means thinking about how it is put together.

Here are some examples of questions like this (all relate to the passage on page 29):

1 Why does the writer use short sentences in the first paragraph and longer ones in the second paragraph?

2 Give one way in which the writer draws the reader in at the beginning.

3 How does the writer create an atmosphere of tension in the first paragraph?

Answering the questions

- Sometimes you just have to give a **reason** for something, e.g. (question 1):

  The short sentences show that Link is tense. The longer sentences in the next paragraph show he is more relaxed.

- Sometimes you need to **refer to the text**, e.g. (question 2):

  The writer says 'he arrived' in the first sentence. We are not told who 'he' is, but we want to know, so this draws us in.

- When you give a quotation, you often need to explain why you have used it. *The writer says 'he arrived' in the first sentence* is not enough on its own, because it doesn't explain the **effect** of the words quoted.

Top Tip!

If the question begins 'How does the author …?', then you are being asked to **explain** the way the author has used words or structure. Back up each point with a quotation from the passage. Make sure you **explain** why the quotation has been used.

Spot Check

1 Why are paragraphs used in a text?
2 Why is the beginning of a text particularly important?

Read the final seven lines of the passage on page 29.

> "Six, seven months," he said. "You?"
>
> "First night."
>
> He chuckled. "I can tell. Where you from?"
>
> "Up north."
>
> "Brum, me."
>
> "I can tell." It was a risk, this crack about his accent, but he only chuckled again. "Name's Ginger," he said, and waited.

Why do the paragraphs suddenly become much shorter at this point? What effect does this have?

Answer

The paragraphs become shorter because the characters are having a conversation. Each speech begins a new line.

Comment

This answer gets half marks. It explains clearly why the writer has used shorter paragraphs, but it doesn't describe the effect of this. To get full marks the student needs to add a comment like this:

It suggests they are talking quickly, in short bursts, especially the very short sentences such as 'First night'.

This includes a quotation from the extract to give an example.

Did You Know?

One short story by Franz Kafka has these famous opening lines:

As Gregor Samsa awoke one morning from uneasy dreams he found himself transformed in his bed into a gigantic insect.

The questions

Some questions ask you to comment on the writer's **use of language** – the **meaning** of certain words, or the **effect** of certain words.
Here are some examples of questions like this (all relate to the passage opposite):

1 In the first sentence, what does 'mischievous little fellow' suggest that the writer feels about frost?

2 What is the effect of describing frost patterns as 'sparkling sculptures' (paragraph 2)?

3 In the whole passage, how does the writer's choice of language make you feel that frost is something attractive?

Answering the questions

• Sometimes your answers will be quite short, e.g. (question 1):

It suggests that the writer thinks frost is fun and plays tricks on us.

• In the longer answers you need to **refer to the text**, e.g. (question 3):

The writer makes you feel frost is attractive by using the image of the artist or sculptor. In the first paragraph he 'paints intricate patterns', and in the third paragraph the patterns are described as 'delicate'. Both of the adjectives 'intricate' and 'delicate' make the patterns sound attractive.

Top Tip!

In your longer answers, it is often a good idea to refer to the words of the question in your answer. For example, the answer to question 3 begins

The writer makes you feel frost is attractive …

This keeps you focused on answering the question, and shows that you are answering the question!

Read this newspaper article. The author explores the legend of Jack Frost and explains how frost affects the landscape.

WEATHERWATCH

Every winter a mischievous little fellow persists in painting intricate patterns on cars, windows, leaves and rocks. Legend has it that Jack Frost was the son of the Norse god of wind, Kari. Originally he was known as Jokul [icicle] Frosti [frost], which became Jack Frost when he emigrated to the UK.

Cold, clear nights with a light wind blowing and temperatures close to freezing are perfect for Jack Frost. Valleys and hollows receive more visits because cold air sinks into low-lying areas. His favourite places to create his sparkling sculptures include rocky, glass or metal surfaces because they radiate heat and cool more quickly than the air surrounding them. Car

windscreens are ideal.

Normally Jack Frost paints delicate, feather-like patterns, otherwise known as hoar frost. He interlocks ice crystals, which grow outwards from a small seed, such as a tiny lump or scratch on the surface. But if the air is moist (often foggy) and the wind a little more breezy then Jack Frost switches to the rime frost technique. Grainy needles grow outwards, lining themselves up with the wind direction and giving structures like electricity pylons a spiky white coat.

Kate Ravilious

(Copyright Guardian Newspapers Limited 2005)

How suitable is the image of a 'spiky white coat' to describe the effect of rime frost (paragraph 3)?

The image describes how a whole structure is covered, like a coat covers a person. It is a white coat because the frost is white.

This answer gets half marks. It explains two features that make the image of the coat fit the description of rime frost, but it doesn't say **how suitable** this image is, e.g.

This makes the image a very suitable one.

The student could also have referred to the 'spiky' frost resembling the material on a coat.

Did YOU Know?

The longest word in the English language is 'smiles'. (There is a mile between the first and last letter!)

Explaining purpose and effect

The questions

Some questions ask you to comment on the **purpose** or **point of view** of the writer. They may also ask you to explain the **effect** of the text.

Here are some examples of questions like this (all relate to the passage on page 35):

1 Suggest a reason why the author begins her explanation of frost by describing the legend of Jack Frost.

2 Does the author like frost? Explain your answer.

3 The writer talks about Jack Frost throughout the article, not frost. What effect does this have?

Answering the questions

- Sometimes your answers will be quite short, e.g. (question 1):

  The author wants to grab the reader's interest at the start with a story.

- In the longer answers you need to **refer to the text**, e.g. (question 2):

  The author seems to like frost a lot. She treats it almost as a person, calling it Jack Frost and saying that 'he' has 'favourite places to create' in. She also describes the effect of frost in a positive way, with adjectives such as 'sparkling' and 'delicate'.

Question

In the passage on page 35 the writer sets out to entertain the reader as well as to explain what frost is.

Give **three** examples of how she entertains the reader, and support each with a quotation.

Give one example from each of these categories:
• the topics covered
• the language used
• the way frost is referred to as Jack Frost.

Top Tip!

The longer questions, which carry more marks, may give a **bullet point list** of topics to include in your answer. To get top marks you need to cover all the suggestions. They can also give you a structure for your answer, if you write a short paragraph on each one.

Answer

The author tells us about the legend of Jack Frost, which is entertaining.

She uses loads of describing words like 'sparkling'.

Frost is referred to as Jack Frost, so he's like a person. He is a 'mischievous little fellow' and he 'paints delicate feather-like patterns'.

level
5

Comment

This is a level 5 answer. It shows some understanding of the purpose of the text, and of how the writer uses different techniques to achieve her purpose. It covers all the three areas suggested in the bullet points. It gives evidence from the text to back up the views.

To raise the level, the student needs to show how the quotations create the effect, e.g.

By saying that Jack Frost 'paints delicate feather-like patterns' the author makes us see frost as an artist who deliberately creates pictures and sculptures. This is an attractive way of describing frost.

Did You Know?

There is a word for the study of bird's eggs: oology (pronounced oh-ology).

If you want to move from level 4 to level 5 you need to show these skills.
(All examples relate to the passage on page 35.)

Understand purpose

You need to think about **why** the text was written. Is it to explain, or tell a story, or persuade you to buy something? Is it a mixture of different purposes? Look at this question and possible answers:

What is the purpose of the article?

To tell you about Jack Frost.

level 4

To tell you about frost in an entertaining way.

level 5

Higher level answers would mention explanation as well as information.

Be aware of how passages are organised

You need to think about the **structure** of the text. How are paragraphs used? Why has it begun and ended as it has? Are there any layout features such as subheadings or boxes of text? Look at this question and possible answers:

Why has the author divided her article into three paragraphs?

Paragraphs are used to show different topics.

level 4

The paragraphs are used to show different topics. The first one talks about the legend of Jack Frost. The others give different kinds of information.

level 5

Higher level answers would point out that the second paragraph describes different places and weather conditions suitable for frost, while the third paragraph describes two different types of frost.

Top Tip!

- Read the question carefully. Answer what the question asks, not what you hope it asks!
- Make sure your quotations are **relevant** to the question asked.

Understand how writers use words to create effects

You need to think about the precise **effect** that certain **words** and phrases have. They will have been chosen deliberately by the writer – why? Look at this question and possible answers:

What is the effect of the phrase 'persists in painting intricate patterns' (lines 2–3)?

It means the frost is always painting clever patterns – you can't stop it.

<table>
<tr><td>level
4</td></tr>
</table>

'Persists' makes it sound as if Jack Frost will do what he wants, and you can't stop him.

<table>
<tr><td>level
5</td></tr>
</table>

> Higher level answers will comment on 'intricate patterns' as well, and on the repeated 'p' sound in the phrase.

Begin to 'read between the lines'

Think about what the writer is aiming to do. The text won't always make this clear. Often you have to work out **opinions** or **feelings** that aren't stated openly. Look at this question and possible answers:

How can you tell that the writer enjoys looking at the effects of frost? Refer to one piece of evidence from the text.

She says that the frost makes patterns.

<table>
<tr><td>level
4</td></tr>
</table>

She describes the frost as making 'delicate, feather-like patterns'.

<table>
<tr><td>level
5</td></tr>
</table>

> Higher level answers will explain why this phrase shows that the writer enjoys frost.

Did YOU Know?

The dot on the letter 'i' is called a tipple.

39

Throughout your Key Stage 3 course, you will be assessed on your writing skills. This section of the book focuses on the different skills you will need to improve your writing and move up a level.

Different types of writing tasks

- Your teacher may give you two different styles of writing tasks to practise. A longer writing task and a shorter writing task.

- Both tasks give you some **background**, and suggest the sort of things you should include in your answer.

- Each writing task will have a different **purpose** and **form**. For example, you may be telling a story, writing a persuasive letter or composing a report.

> *Pages 52–3 (different forms) and 62–71 (different purposes).*

What you get marks for

- **Composition and effect**
  This means making your language and style interesting and varied. It also means writing to suit the audience and purpose given.

> *Pages 42–3, 46–9 and 52–3.*

- **Sentence structure and punctuation**
  This means how well organised and varied your sentences are, and whether you have used punctuation correctly.

> *Pages 48–9 and 54–7.*

- **Text structure and organisation**
  This means how well organised your whole text is, e.g. use of paragraphs and the order of your points.

> *Pages 50–1.*

- **Spelling**
  This is marked only in the shorter writing task.

> *Pages 58–61.*

Top Tip!
Try hard to spell words correctly – it could push you from a level 4 to a level 5.

Timing and planning

- You should spend the first 15 minutes **planning** your longer writing task.

- You should spend the last 5 minutes **checking** what you have written – improving the spelling, punctuation and vocabulary.

> *Pages 44–5.*

Section A
Longer writing task
Building progress

You work for a company that is building a new leisure centre. Your manager has sent you this memo:

Please report on progress so far. Write a detailed report explaining:

- how the different sports and leisure facilities are progressing (quality and speed)
- how well the construction workers are addressing the task
- whether you see any problems with the leisure centre at this stage.

Write a report for your manager explaining what progress is being made in building the leisure centre.

30 marks

This shows you that it is a **longer task**, so you will probably need about 45 minutes to do this sample question.

A bit of **scene setting** to give you the background to the task and your role.

This tells you what the **task** is.

Did YOU Know?

A **blend** is a word made up of the shortened form of two other words, e.g. **heli**port (**heli**copter + air**port**).

Spot Check

True or false?
1 You should write as much as possible.
2 You get extra marks for correct spelling.
3 Text structure and organisation is about your handwriting.

Ask yourself: What am I writing?

- Look at the **format** word in the question paper, e.g. Write a **letter**, an **account**, the first chapter of your **story**, a **leaflet**.

- Keep this format in mind as you plan and write. Most formats have special **rules**.

Pages 52–3.

- Now identify the **content**, or **topic**, that you have to write about, e.g. (a letter) describing your **visit**, or (a report) describing your **project**.

Ask yourself: Why am I writing?

- Work out your **purpose** in writing.

- **Stories** are easy – they should entertain.

- For non-fiction, though, you must look for the key word in the question. This might be: **inform**, **explain**, **describe**, **persuade**, **argue**, **advise**, **analyse**, **review** or **comment**. Understanding the purpose of the writing will mean you approach it in the right way.

Pages 66–71.

Top Tip!

Always keep **purpose**, **audience** and **role** in mind while you are planning and writing your answers. You need to keep a consistent 'viewpoint' to get a level 5.

Ask yourself: Who am I writing for?

- Keep your **audience** in mind when you plan and write. You have to adjust what you are writing to suit what they want to read.

- The audience is not the examiners, but the **person** (or people) indicated **in the question**, e.g. your fellow classmates, the head teacher, the prime minister, the manager of a factory.

Ask yourself: What is my role?

You will often be told to imagine you are a **particular person**, e.g. a resident of a certain place, a head teacher, a newspaper reporter. This is your 'role'. **Get in role** and keep in role. This means:

- not changing your **point of view**, e.g. from student to teacher, or from 3rd person to 1st person.

- not changing the **formality** of the language, e.g. from formal to informal, unless for deliberate effect.

Pages 26–7.

- not changing the **tone**, e.g. from light-hearted to serious.

Example

Look again at the writing task from page 41.

How does thinking about purpose, audience and role help you approach the task?

**Section A
Longer writing task
Building progress**

You work for a company that is building a new leisure centre. Your manager has sent you this memo:

Please report on progress so far. Write a detailed report explaining:
- how the different sports and leisure facilities are progressing (quality and speed)
- how well the construction workers are addressing the task
- whether you see any problems with the leisure centre at this stage.

Write a report for your manager explaining what progress is being made in building the leisure centre.

30 marks

This is your **role** – you work for a building company. You need to keep this role going through the writing.

This list suggests the **content** of your report. You could **organise** the report into three sections like this.

In the task, you are given:
- the **form** of the writing (a report)
- the **purpose** of the writing (to explain)
- the **audience** of the writing (your manager).
So the report should be clear, formal, logical and polite.

Did You Know?

The most common word used in conversation is 'I'.

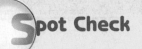

Spot Check

Match the question with the correct purpose.

Question	Purpose
1 Give your views on …	To inform or describe
2 Tell x how to …	To persuade
3 Give an account of …	To instruct
4 Inspire your team …	To argue

Planning is important

- You must spend time planning the answers to both writing tasks.

- Planning makes you **think carefully** about the task, instead of writing the first thing that comes into your head.

- It improves the **content** of your writing. You have time to think up good ideas.

- It also improves the **structure** of your writing. You can organise it instead of just rambling on.

Planning for the longer task

- If you are doing a longer task, then it's good practice to spend **at least 15 minutes** planning your answer.

- Your teacher may give you a planning grid, which will often supply the basic structure for your writing.

Top Tip!

Read carefully the **detail** given in the background to the question. It will give you lots of ideas for:
(a) what to write about
(b) how to structure your answer.

Planning for the shorter task

- You are not given a planning page for the shorter writing task. However, make sure you spend at least 5 minutes **thinking and planning** before you start writing.

Pages 64–71 (planning tools).

- You can use the question paper or some spare paper to draw up a **quick plan**.

- **Brainstorm** some key words and ideas first. Then develop these ideas and put them into a sensible order.

Spot Check

True or false?
1 You should start writing as soon as you can.
2 You should spend at least 5 minutes planning for the shorter writing task.
3 Planning helps you organise your writing more effectively.

This is a planning page for the question:

Write the beginning of a short story about someone who has been left on their own.

> **You may wish to use this page to plan your work.**
> (This page will not be marked.)
>
> | **Notes for description of character** | **Notes for description of setting** |
> | --- | --- |
> | - astronaut – unnamed (1st person)
- normally cool and calm
- dressed in full gear, heavy helmet, etc. | - space station
- set in future, 2500
- huge area, lots of levels
- vast banks of computers
- completely empty – very eerie
- station circling a new, black planet |
>
> **Notes on what happens in the story**
> - I wake up, after a year's 'frozen' sleep
> - all companions gone – feelings of being alone
> - explore space station, signs that it was left in a hurry – why?
> - computer tells me we're being sucked into dark planet

This planning page helps you gather ideas for a **story**.

The notes are **short** and **simple**.

Jot ideas in the boxes as they occur to you.

Only this panel can be used to **structure** the story.

Did YOU Know?

Charles Dickens was involved in one of the first train crashes in history, when his train plunged over a bridge in 1864. Many people died, and the author never recovered from the experience.

A **wide vocabulary** helps your writing in many ways:

It makes it more interesting

- Adjectives and adverbs improve your descriptions, e.g.
  He lay the axe on the ground. ✗
  He lay his battered axe wearily on the ground. ✓

- Longer, more difficult words are often impressive, e.g.
  an atrocious attack, un unacceptable request.

It makes it more precise

- Try to avoid nouns and verbs that are very general, e.g.
  She ran to the shops. ✗
  She jogged all the way to the newsagent's on the corner. ✓

- The exact noun or verb you use creates a particular effect:
  The cat lounged in the summer house.
  The cat whimpered in the shed.

It makes it more suitable

Choose words to suit the purpose and audience of your writing:

- more **formal** words for a discussion piece, e.g. *locate, conclusion*

- some **informal** words for a teenage audience, e.g. *cool, kids*

- **emotive** words in persuasive writing, e.g. *broken-hearted, abandoned*

- **technical** words in information writing, e.g. *species, habitat*

Top Tip!

When you are checking through your work, don't be afraid to cross words out and replace them with better ones. You will get marks for using a higher level word, even if it is spelt incorrectly.

Spot Check

1 Think of four alternatives for the word 'bad'.
2 Rank them in order of 'badness' (the worst at the end).
3 Which of these words would you **not** use in a formal discussion?
wonderful, spectacular, fab, delightful, stimulating

This is a level 5 student's review.

Read the examiner's comments on the vocabulary used.

level
5

Philip Pullman has written a <u>great</u> end to 'His Dark Materials' trilogy – 'The Amber Spyglass', which is just as well written as 'Northern Lights' and 'The Subtle Knife' – the first two titles in the <u>trilogy</u>. The conflict in the other books gets <u>bigger</u> and <u>bigger</u> and seems to involve the whole universe.

Will and Lyra have become separated, they are being hunted down by <u>terrible powers</u>, and they are trying to find each other and their friends. Will and Lyra are the two main <u>characters</u>. They are <u>beautifully drawn</u> characters, and I nearly cried at the end.

It's a <u>great</u> adventure story, and goes at a <u>great</u> <u>pace</u>, with lots of <u>twists and turns</u>. All the characters from the rest of the trilogy are involved such as Lord Asriel, Mrs Coulter, and my favourite Iorek Byrnison the king of the armoured bears. Will and Lyra are the most important characters, however, as I've said.

The language of the book is difficult at times, but it's still a fantastic story which beats 'Harry Potter' and even 'Lord of The Rings'.

Comment

Some **precise** and **interesting** words and phrases used, such as *terrible powers*, *beautifully drawn* and *twists and turns*. Some **technical terms** appropriate for a review used (*pace*, *trilogy*, *characters*). However, the adjectives often **lack variety and power**, such as *great* and *bigger*.

Did You Know?

The English word with the largest number of meanings is 'set'. One English dictionary lists 58 uses of 'set' as a noun and 126 uses as a verb.

Making your sentences interesting

Vary the type of your sentences

- Most sentences are **statements**, e.g. *The CD cost £14.99.*

- You can add **variety** by including other types of sentence:
  - **questions**, e.g. *How much does this CD cost?* (Note the question mark.)
  - **exclamations**, e.g. *Only £14.99!* (Note the exclamation mark.)
  - **commands**, e.g. *Buy this CD for me!*

Vary the length of your sentences

- **Short sentences** often have only one clause, e.g.
  Tammy borrowed £5 from her brother.
  They are useful in instructions and straightforward information text.

- **Longer sentences** combine clauses with 'and' or 'but', e.g.
  Tammy borrowed £5 from her brother and didn't pay him back.
  Don't construct too many sentences like this: *… and … and … and then …*

- Combine clauses in different ways to make sentences **more precise** and **more interesting**.
  - Use **connectives** such as 'although' and 'when', e.g. *Tammy borrowed £5 from her brother since she had left her purse behind.*
  - Include **relative** clauses (which …, who …, that …) to add information, e.g. *Tammy borrowed £5 from her brother, who never let her forget it.*

Other kinds of variety

- **Begin** your sentences in different ways:
  He went to the arcade. He played on the games. He … ✗
  He went to the arcade. After he'd played on the games, he … ✓

- Expand your nouns with **noun phrases**:
  She was given an alarm clock. ✗
  She was given an alarm clock designed to leap about instead of making a sound. ✓

Top Tip!
Remember that every sentence must make sense on its own. This almost always means that every sentence has a verb.

Did You Know?
You should never write 'would of' or 'should of'. The correct form is 'would have' or 'should have', e.g. *I would have got full marks.*

Look again at the level 5 student's review from page 47. This time, concentrate on the **sentence structure**.

level 5

Philip Pullman has written a great end to 'His Dark Materials' trilogy – 'The Amber Spyglass', which is just as well written as 'Northern Lights' and 'The Subtle Knife' – the first two titles in the trilogy. The conflict in the other books gets bigger and bigger and seems to involve the whole universe.

Will and Lyra have become separated, they are being hunted down by terrible powers, and they are trying to find each other and their friends. Will and Lyra are the two main characters. They are beautifully drawn characters, and I nearly cried at the end.

It's a great adventure story, and goes at a great pace, with lots of twists and turns. All the characters from the rest of the trilogy are involved such as Lord Asriel, Mrs Coulter, and my favourite Iorek Byrnison the king of the armoured bears. Will and Lyra are the most important characters, however, as I've said.

The language of the book is difficult at times, but it's still a fantastic story which beats 'Harry Potter' and even 'Lord of The Rings'.

Good points:
– includes relative clauses to add information;
– clauses have been added to make sentences longer;
– some noun phrases and connectives add interest and detail.

Could improve by:
– avoiding using too many dashes to add information;
– avoiding beginning sentences with the same words;
– combining clauses using connectives other than 'and'.

Spot Check Combine these sentences to make them more interesting: *Kevin took the bus to town. He didn't want to miss the start of the film. He pushed through the crowds.*

The key things you need to know

- A paragraph is a group of sentences on one topic. Paragraphs are used to **organise** your writing and to help the reader **follow your ideas**.

- You begin a new paragraph when you talk about a **new point**, **character**, **place** or **time**.

- You show it's a new paragraph by leaving a line space, or starting the new line slightly in from the margin.

Ordering paragraphs

- This is where **planning** is vital. Each main item in your plan will often become a separate paragraph.

Pages 44–5.

- Number the items on your plan to give you a **sensible order** for your paragraphs.

- The **first paragraph** must grab the reader's attention. (In some non-fiction texts, it may be a general introduction.)

- Your **final paragraph** must be a definite ending.

Top Tip!

When checking your work, you can use an insertion mark and write ⓃⓅ, where you want to start a new paragraph.

Signalling where you are going

- Use **topic sentences** to start each paragraph. These give the main point of the paragraph. Then develop the point by adding reasons, examples, etc.

- Show where your sentences are going by using **connectives**, e.g. *Yet …* (= here's an opposite point), and **signposts**, e.g. *The following day …* (= to tell you when) and *Other people disagree …* (= to tell you who).

Spot Check

1 Give two reasons why you would start a new paragraph.
2 'You need a new paragraph every 10 or 15 lines.' True or false?
3 Explain what a topic sentence is.

This example of an advice text gains a level 5 for its organisation and structure.

level
5

How to deal with rejection

When a relationship breaks up, it can be a very painful experience, especially if it happens quickly. You can feel a shock, almost as if your friend has died.

If the relationship was a really good one, it's normal to feel grief that it's over. So don't think that it's wrong to get some of the grief out of your system by having a good cry. If the relationship is clearly over, don't waste time trying to patch it up. If you go round pleading with your ex-boyfriend/girlfriend to take you back, you're only prolonging the agony. You're more likely to turn them off than win them back.

Finally, don't worry that you'll never make another relationship. When a relationship ends, it can be difficult to think there'll be others. But there will be!

Also, one thing people do when they're rejected is to ask themselves what went wrong. Remember that relationships end for all sorts of reasons, and it's hardly ever one person's fault.

Logical point to put at the beginning. ✓

Main point given first (topic sentence), then developed. ✓

Need a new paragraph here, as it's a new point. ✗

This paragraph would be better at the end. ✗

Connectives show how the ideas are linked. ✓

Sob

Did You Know?

The Unfortunates (1969) is a novel supplied in a box. Its author, Bryan Johnson, provides the first and last chapters but presents the rest as single pages that can be read in any order.

Letters

- **Lay out** the letter properly.

Page 53.

- Most letters need a **formal** style, e.g. a letter of complaint, a letter to a newspaper, or to apply for a job.

- Some letters will be more **informal**, e.g. a letter to a friend or relative.

Pages 26–7 (formality).

Newspaper stories

- Write in a **clear but lively** style. Use **short paragraphs** and **short sentences**.

- The first paragraph often gives the main information – answering the questions 'who', 'what', 'where' and 'when'. Later paragraphs give further details.

- Include **quotes** from people involved, or comments from experts, e.g. *Ben Potts, a neighbour, said, "…".*

- Add a snappy **headline**.

Top Tip!

When writing a leaflet, don't waste time on design. For example, draw an empty box and add a label (*picture of …*) rather than spending time drawing an actual picture.

Leaflets

- **Presentation** – include bullet points and subheadings to break up the text. Leave spaces for graphics, pictures or logos.

- **Structure** – use short paragraphs and sentences. Include headings to guide the reader through the text.

- **Style** – use clear and simple language for information or advice leaflets. Include persuasive techniques if you are selling a product or an idea.

Pages 70–1.

Reports

- Most reports are **factual** and **formal**, like a school report. They use clear and formal language, and a reasonable tone.

- **Impersonal phrases** and **passive verbs** are common, e.g. *It is preferable …* or *The product was assessed …*

- Give it a **logical structure** – an introduction, then the main points in order of importance, and a summary at the end.

Did You Know?

One of the shortest letters was written by the novelist Victor Hugo. Wanting to know how people were reacting to his latest novel, he wrote to his publishers: '?' They replied: '!'

Speeches

- Remember that the audience will be **listening** to the speech, so try and imagine someone reading it aloud. Some good **sound effects** include:
  - **repetition**, e.g. *It's time to protest, and to protest with force.*
  - **alliteration**, e.g. *The proposal is dangerous and destructive.*
  - **lists of three**, e.g. *… for a better, fairer and more prosperous future.*

- Vary the length of your sentences for effect.

Pages 48–9.

Example

Note how this letter is set out.

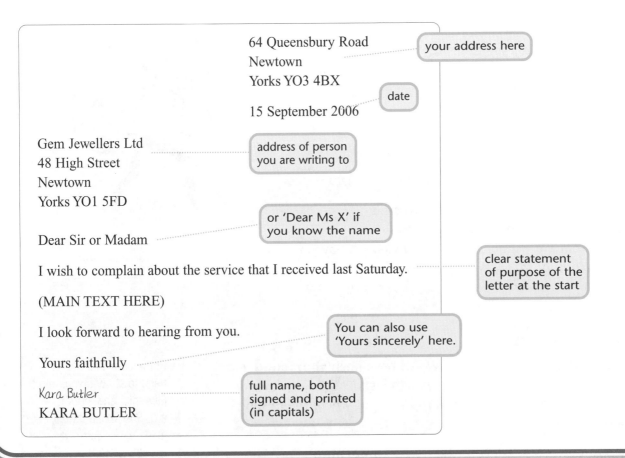

64 Queensbury Road
Newtown
Yorks YO3 4BX

`your address here`

15 September 2006

`date`

Gem Jewellers Ltd
48 High Street
Newtown
Yorks YO1 5FD

`address of person you are writing to`

Dear Sir or Madam

`or 'Dear Ms X' if you know the name`

I wish to complain about the service that I received last Saturday.

`clear statement of purpose of the letter at the start`

(MAIN TEXT HERE)

I look forward to hearing from you.

`You can also use 'Yours sincerely' here.`

Yours faithfully

Kara Butler
KARA BUTLER

`full name, both signed and printed (in capitals)`

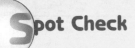

Spot Check

Which of these phrases would you include in a letter, and which would you include in a speech?
1 With reference to your advert …
2 Are we so bad? Are we so mad?
3 Dear Sir
4 I stand before you this evening …
5 I look forward to hearing from you

Basic rules

- Every sentence must make complete sense on its own, so it must contain a verb:
  - *Twenty minutes on the trampoline.* ✗
  - *She was on the trampoline for 20 minutes.* ✓

- Every sentence must begin with a **capital letter**.

- Capitals are also used for **proper names**, e.g. *Raj, Ipswich, Nike, Robston College.*

- Every sentence must **end** with a **full stop**, a **question mark** or an **exclamation mark**:
  - *Steve is running.* (statement)
  - *Run, Steve!* (exclamation or command)
  - *Why don't you run, Steve?* (question)

Punctuation for adding text

- A **dash** adds a short bit of information, e.g.
  I put it here – no, here.
  Do not overuse dashes.

- A **colon** introduces a list, e.g.
  These are our demands: £10,000 in cash, a getaway car …

- You can **mark off extra information** by using dashes, brackets or commas:
  The culprit – or so it appeared – had slipped away.
  The culprit (or so it appeared) had slipped away.

Pages 56–7.

Apostrophes

- An apostrophe is used where words have been **shortened**, e.g. *haven't* (have not), *I'm* (I am), *he's* (he is), *let's* (let us), *they're* (they are). Note that the apostrophe is put where the missing letter should be.

- Apostrophes also tell you who **owns something**:
  - for **singular**, add apostrophe + **s**, e.g. *Brett's car, United's win*
  - for **plural**, add the apostrophe after the **s**, e.g. *a friends' gathering*

- Do not confuse apostrophes with speech marks.

Top Tip!

Remember that 'its' is used to show ownership (like 'his' and 'hers'), e.g. *She pulled its tail.*
'It's' stands for 'it is', e.g. *It's raining.*

Example

This level 4 writing has some correct punctuation, but needs to improve to get a level 5.

level
4

> Have you heard people say that soaps are just like real life They are'nt nearly as realistic as real life, for several reasons – first of all, people die (or disappear) far more often in soaps. This is because of the actor's desire to leave the series after a period. If a key figure wants to leave, the producer has only two option's. One is to kill him off and the other is divorce. Also theres always something happening in characters lives in soaps in real life its actually quite boring.

Question mark missing.

You need to start a new sentence here.

Incorrect use of apostrophe.

Did You Know?

The wrong use of an apostrophe in words that are just plurals is known as the 'greengrocer's apostrophe'. This is because it is so common to see signs like this at greengrocers' stalls.

Apple's half price

Spot Check

1 When do you need to use a capital letter?
2 Add the punctuation:
   graemes mobile rang it was paula calling from oxford
3 Correct the punctuation:
   'Its endless is'nt it!' she said – looking at: the minute's go by.

55

What is a comma?

The comma is a very useful and common punctuation mark. It is used in many different ways to **separate words**, **phrases and clauses** in a sentence. Using the comma well in your writing shows:
– that you can organise your sentences, so that their meaning is clear.
– that you can use punctuation accurately.

Separating words and phrases

- The comma must be used to **separate items in a list**:
  Please put all clothes, books, swimming and sporting equipment, mobile phones and other personal belongings in the lockers provided.
  Note that the final item before 'and' (*mobile phones*) does not need a comma after it.

- The comma is used to **separate a phrase** that gives extra information about something:
  The third from the right, the woman in the hat, is the winner!

Separating the main parts of a sentence

- The comma is used to **separate the main parts of a sentence**:
  Although Keith ran as fast as he could, he still came last.
  Rebecca agreed to look after the dog, which was the worst decision she had ever made.

Avoiding the comma

- Think about what really links the clauses of a sentence. Often using a comma is not the best form of punctuation:
  To display web pages you need software called a browser, this converts the coded pages into a form that you can read on the computer.
  Here the second clause is just 'tagged on'. You should use a **colon** instead of a comma, or start a new sentence:
  To display web pages you need software called a browser. This converts the coded pages into a form that you can read on the computer.

Do not overuse commas. Think about using other punctuation marks as well.

Example

Look at how one student has used commas in this piece of writing.

level
5

Lots of girls want to look like the celebrities they see on TV, but celebrities have to look amazing, it's what they are paid to do. Unlike ordinary people, they have the time and money to achieve that perfect look. Most of the girls you see around town, would look just as fantastic if they had personal trainers, beauticians, stylists and dieticians at their fingertips. Remember too that celebrities use top photographers, who are trained to get the best out of their subject. So don't judge your looks against photographs of top models: it simply isn't a fair comparison.

Colon or dash would be better than a comma here. ✗

No comma needed here. ✗

Comma separates items in a list. ✓

Comma used to separate clauses. ✓

Colon better than a comma here. ✓

Comment

This is a level 5 piece of writing. Commas are mostly used accurately and effectively. They show the structure of the sentences clearly. Other punctuation is sometimes used instead of commas where necessary.

Did YOU Know?

The final chapter of James Joyce's novel *Ulysses* consists of eight enormous sentences. It goes on for over 60 pages and has no punctuation.

Spot Check

Add commas to these sentences:
1 He used the colours red white yellow and blue.
2 Lucy the youngest of the children is really the most important character.
3 Stuart was replaced at half-time which was the final straw.

57

WRITING — Spelling: endings and beginnings

Plurals

Add **-s** to make the plural of a word, e.g. *house → houses, pool → pools*.

Exceptions:

- Words ending in **-ss**, **-sh**, **-ch**, **-x**: you add **-es**, e.g. *glasses, matches, foxes.*

- Words ending in consonant + **y**: you change **-y** to **-ies**, e.g. *lady → ladies, try → tries.*

- Words ending in **-f**: you usually change **-f** to **-ves**, e.g. *loaf → loaves, leaf → leaves.*

- Some words don't follow these rules, e.g. *children, women, mice, sheep.*

Verbs

Add **-ing** or **-ed** to make different parts of the verb, e.g. *form → forming, formed; watch → watching, watched.*

Exceptions:

- Short verbs ending in vowel + consonant: you double the consonant, e.g. *drop → dropping, dropped; fit → fitting, fitted.*

- Verbs ending in **-e**: you drop the **-e**, e.g. *decide → deciding, decided; state → stating, stated.*

- Many common verbs have different forms in the past tense, e.g. *fight → fought, begin → began, meet → met.*

Prefixes and suffixes

- **Prefixes** are letters added at the **start** of a word to change its meaning:

  - **in-**, **un-**, **im-**, **ir-**, **mis-** and **dis-** often form opposites, e.g. *invisible, unfair, impossible, mistrust.*
  - **pre-** and **fore-** mean 'in front' or 'before', e.g. *prefer, foreground.*

- Prefixes do not change the spelling of the original word.

- **Suffixes** are letters added at the **end** of a word to change its meaning:

  - **-able**, **-ible** and **-uble** mean that something is possible, e.g. *legible, soluble.*
  - **-ful** means 'full of', e.g. *careful, peaceful.* (Note: not **-full**.)

- You drop a final **-e** before a suffix that begins with a vowel, e.g. *forgive + -able = forgivable*

Example

Look at this extract from a level 4 answer to a shorter writing task.

> I don't beleive in horroscopes at all. No one knowes about the future but <u>Allah</u>. Sometimes they come true but I think that it's considence. On Wendnesday the horoscope said: "Something bad will happen today". I worryed all day, and then I cought a cold. But surley everyday there's something bad that happens!

level
4

The student checked her spelling at the end of the test and made these corrections, which took her answer up to a level 5.

> I don't believe in horoscopes at all. No one knows about the future but <u>Allah</u>. Sometimes they come true but I think that it's coincidence. On Wednesday the horoscope said: "Something bad will happen today". I worried all day, and then I caught a cold. But surely every day there's something bad that happens!

level
5

Did You Know?

'Dreamt' is the only English word ending in 'mt'.

Spot Check

1 Which are the incorrect plurals?
   churches, potatoes, flys, wolves, gasses
2 Add **-ing** and **-ed** to these verbs:
   skate, skid, respect
3 Give the past tense of these verbs:
   find, steal, travel, buy

Use a dictionary

- The best way to master spelling is to look words up in a **dictionary** while you are writing.

- Do *not* use spell checker programs. They make you a lazy speller.

- Note: you are not allowed to use a dictionary in the tests.

Collins
Easy Learning
English
Dictionary

The easiest way to succeed in English

List your spelling bugs

- **Make a list** of words you regularly misspell. Make a bookmark out of it. Learn them.

- **Learn** these commonly misspelt words:
  all right
  believe
  character
  clothes
  coming
  definite
  friend
  quiet
  receive
  separate

Sob

friend
A ~~freind~~ in need ...

> **Top Tip!**
> You will get credit for using a complicated word in your test, even if you misspell it.

Beware of homophones

- Some common words **sound the same** but are spelt differently. Learn these and look out for others:

  - *their* (belonging to them), *they're* (= they are), *there* (where)

  - *wear* (clothes), *we're* (= we are), *where* (here), *were* (past tense of are)

  - *are* (present tense of were), *our* (belonging to us)

  - *to* (go to bed), *too* (much), *two* (2)

  - *whose* (belonging to someone), *who's* (= who is)

whose
~~Who's~~ clothes are these?

Other spelling tips

- Learn a few **spelling rules**.

Pages 58–9.

- Use **memory joggers**, e.g. Remember there is **iron** in the env**iron**ment, a **rat** in sepa**rat**e, **finite** in de**finite** and a **cog** in re**cog**nise.

- **Say the word** in your mind as it is spelt, e.g. Fe**bru**ary, Wed**nes**day.

- Break words into smaller chunks, e.g. *ex-treme-ly, re-le-vant*.

A student has checked this paragraph and corrected the spelling in places. Read the paragraph and the examiner's comment.

level
4

> Bad behaveour basicly doesn't start in the classroom, it starts in sociatey. You're not going to be naughty ~~naugthy~~) in school for no reason. Exclusion isn't a good idea – it's just like giving them a holiday. They should keep them in school longer really, at weekends. If the kid has broken the law then the police ~~aught~~ ought to definately be involved, but if no crime is ~~commited~~ committed bad behaveour is just a matter for the school.

Comment

Spelling of simple words is correct. Some common longer words are accurately spelt, e.g. *involved, committed*. But some words are misspelt – *basicly* (basically), *behaveour* (behaviour), *sociatey* (society), *definately* (definitely) – so 2 out of 4 marks are awarded.

Did YOU Know?

The first printers added letters to the ends of words to straighten the right-hand edge of their texts. Spelling wasn't so important in the Middle Ages!

Spot Check

1 Which of these words are spelt incorrectly?
   quietly, dissappoint, believe, friend, wierd, necessary, ocasion
2 What is the difference between *their* and *there*?
3 Give a memory jogger that helps you spell.

Planning and structure

- You need to plan the **structure** of your story carefully:

  - Give your story a **beginning** (when you introduce the plot/setting/characters), a **middle** (when you develop plot and character) and an **ending** (when things are sorted out, or you keep the reader guessing with a cliffhanger).

  - If you want a **fast moving** story, make it exciting and full of tension.

  - If you want a **slow moving** story, focus more on character, feelings and description.

Pages 44–5.

Top Tip!

Before you begin writing, think about how you are going to end your story. A cliffhanger ending is deliberate – it isn't just an ending that tails off.

Characters

- Your characters need to be **believable** and **interesting**. Don't include more than two or three.

- Describe characters by how they **look**, what they **say** and what they **do**. Often their feelings are better **implied** than stated directly:
  The children felt very cold. ✗
  The children huddled together, their teeth chattering. ✓

- Get **under the skin** of the main character and write from their point of view.

- Keep your **viewpoint consistent**. If you begin writing as the main character (using 'I'), stick to it.

Shiver

Speech

- Speech adds variety to your story. It also **develops the characters and the plot** and brings both to life.

- Make speech **realistic**. People speak in short sentences and use slang. Think how *you* would speak in that situation.

- Follow the rules for **punctuating** speech, and other guidelines.

Page 63.

Language

- Make your sentences **interesting**. Think carefully about the words that you use. In particular:

  – Use **adjectives** and **adverbs** to give descriptive detail, especially to create the setting.

Page 18 (imagery) and pages 48–9 (variety).

  – Use powerful **nouns** and **verbs** for effect.

  – Include some **imagery**.

  – **Vary** the length and type of your sentences.

Example

Follow these guidelines when writing dialogue.

Begin a new paragraph each time the speaker changes.	Put speech marks around the words that are spoken.

The policeman grabbed Keith by the collar. "Not so fast, lad," he whispered in his ear.

"Ow, leggo!" yelled Keith. "I ain't done nothin'."

Jim heard the commotion and turned back. "It's all right, officer," he called reassuringly. "I can explain everything."

Vary your words for 'said'.

Note how Keith's speech is informal, but Jim's is formal.

Did YOU Know?

The initials of J R R Tolkien, the author of *Lord of the Rings*, stand for John Ronald Reuel.

Spot Check

1 What is the basic structure for a story?
2 'The more characters the better.' True or false?
3 Give two rules to follow when including dialogue.

The key things you need to know

- You may be asked to describe an **event**, **place** or **person**. Your aim is to tell the readers about it in an interesting and entertaining way.

- Descriptions mean giving more than the facts. You have to **bring the event, person or place to life** by using language effectively.

Planning and structure

- A **spider diagram** is good for planning description. Brainstorm **different ideas** on the subject. Then decide on the **order**.

- Start with the main idea in the middle and branch out like this:

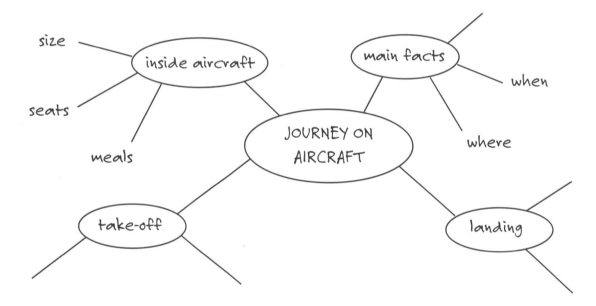

Descriptive language

- Use the **senses**. Describe what you see, smell, hear, touch, taste and feel, e.g.
  I jumped as the elephant lifted its trunk and bellowed.

- Use **powerful words** instead of dull words, e.g.
  The town was full of rang with the cries of street sellers.

- Include some special **imagery** if you can, e.g.
  His eyebrows scuttled like spiders across his brow.

- Go into **detail**. Precise description is more powerful than general comments, e.g.
  I put on my hat thick green bobble hat and opened the door.

- **Vary** the length and type of your sentences.

> **Top Tip!**
> The description does *not* have to be true, but it has to be believable.

Page 18.

Pages 48–9.

Example

This is the beginning of a description of 'a memorable journey'. Read the comments on the good points, and on the things that would improve the writing.

My first trip on an aeroplane was when I was about six. We were going on holiday to Spain, just like millions of other people, but it was a new experience for me.

Everything was strange, even before we got on the aircraft I could see vast halls full of people. Our suitcases disappeared behind some flaps, like they were being eaten by a mechanical monster. There were lots of officials in uniform who always knew where they were going.

Structure is careful and clear. 1st paragraph gives the background. ✓

Language could be more lively and interesting, e.g. 'Our destination was …' ✗

Description in the 2nd paragraph conveys writer's feeling of being overwhelmed.
Good simile of monster. ✓

Could replace some dull words, e.g. 'got on' with 'boarded', 'could see' with 'was transfixed by'. 'Everything was strange' would make a powerful 1st sentence on its own. ✗

Did YOU Know?

A cliché is a phrase that has been over-used, which makes it dull and lifeless. Examples are 'take the bull by the horns' and 'a blessing in disguise'.

Spot Check

1 Give one reason why a spider diagram is useful for planning descriptions.
2 Why are adjectives useful in descriptive writing?
3 What is imagery?

Writing to inform and explain

Structure and planning

- Spider diagrams are useful planning tools when writing **information**.

Page 64.

- A step-by-step planning tool works well when writing **explanation** texts e.g.

Introduction ⟶ Step 1 ⟶ Step 2

- Use **paragraphs** to organise your writing – one paragraph for each bubble on the diagram.

- Use **connectives** to guide the reader through the text and link the paragraphs, e.g. *first, then, in addition, for example, because, as a result, when, therefore.*

- Begin with a clear **introduction**.

Content and language

- Information and explanation texts are mainly **facts**. They need to be **clear**. Avoid persuasive or very descriptive language.

- Use **formal** English, in the **3rd person** (unless the facts are about you):
  I hang out in a youth club, but there's another one too. ✗
  Teenagers have the choice of two youth clubs. ✓

Pages 42 and 46.

Top Tip!

Remember your **audience** when writing. Children will need a different approach to (say) parents or older people.

- Begin each paragraph with a **general statement** (topic sentence), then continue with further **detail** or **examples**, e.g.
  Animals can do some extraordinary things. Pumas, for example, can jump up to 20 metres.

Pages 50–1.

This is an extract from an information sheet that a student wrote about their own house, for a 'time capsule'. Read the comments on the good points, and on the things that would improve the writing.

It was built in the 1890s from Cotswold stone. The house is attached to both its neighbours, forming a terrace of three. There is plenty of space for a family of five, it is spread over four floors. The ground floor consists of a small entrance hall which leads to a double-sized living room with an open fire, piano and hi-fi.

At one end (of the ground floor) is a large kitchen extension. At the other is a south-facing conservatory with a sofa and TV. There is a downstairs toilet.

On the first floor is a large single bedroom and a bathroom with a walk-in shower ...

Better to begin with the subject: 'The house, built in the 1890s, …' ✗

Better to begin a new paragraph with 'The ground floor', as it's a new topic. ✗

Very factual, lots of nouns – not trying to 'sell' house to a buyer. ✓

Needs some connectives to guide reader, e.g. 'also', 'in addition'. ✗

All formal and consistently in the 3rd person. ✓

New topic, so new paragraph. ✓

Did YOU Know?

English borrows from many other languages, e.g. *hamburger* (German), *kayak* (Eskimo) and *shampoo* (Hindi).

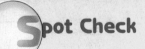

Spot Check

1 'The main aim of an information text is to entertain the reader.' True or false?
2 Why is a step-by-step planning tool useful for explanation texts?
3 Give three connectives that you might use in an information or explanation text.

Writing to discuss and review

Structure and planning

- A spider diagram is a useful planning tool for a **review**. Give each feature of the book, film, etc. a different bubble, e.g.
  - for a **book**: plot, characters, language, themes
  - for a **film**: plot, acting, special effects, direction

Page 64.

- Begin with **information** about the product, then **one paragraph per feature**, then **sum up** your view.

- Use the planning tool on the right for a balanced **discussion**.

1 Introduction to issue: ——————————————	
2 Points for ———————————— ————————————	3 Points against ———————————— ————————————
4 Conclusion – summing up (include your view) —————————————————————	

- Use **connectives** to guide the reader through the discussion, e.g. *therefore, in addition, on the other hand, however.*

- Make it clear **who holds what views**, e.g. *Other people say …, Opponents argue …*

Language and style

- In **discussion** texts:

  - use **formal** language, e.g. *A view shared by many is that …*

  - give **examples** and **quote** people's views, e.g.
    Sandra, for example, says, 'Smokers should pay for their own hospital bills.' (direct speech)
    Sandra believes that smokers should pay for their own hospital bills. (indirect speech)

  - present people's views **fairly** – put your own view in the **conclusion**.

- In **reviews**:

  - your style can be more **lively and informal**, e.g. *Flip to the end and you'll get a shock.*

  - cover both the **good and bad points** of the product.

  - include your **own view** throughout, e.g. *I felt that …*

  - write in the **present tense**, e.g. *The special effects are amazing, the characters fail to convince.*

Top Tip!

In a discussion piece, it is OK to make up the evidence (people's views), as long as it is realistic.

SMOKERS SHOULD PAY FOR THEIR OWN HOSPITAL BILLS.

Pages 47 and 49 (reviews).

Example

This is the start of a discussion which analyses the results of a survey on attitudes to single-sex schools. Read the comments on the good points, and on the things that would improve the writing.

Both parents and students are deeply divided on the issue, as this survey shows.

It's mostly girls who say 'yes' to single-sex schools, like Louise, who says 'They allow students to learn, without getting distracted by boys'. And I think you can 'be yourself' more at an all-girls school. But some boys like them too. For example, Greg says you can see girls plenty after school.

Others, like Yajnah, are anti. They think ...

Structure:

- first paragraph is introduction
- one paragraph for each set of views
- connectives used to guide reader, e.g. 'but', 'for example' ✓

- introduction needs to say what the issue is: single-sex schools ✗

Language/style:

- mostly formal language (but see below)
- mostly a balanced approach (but see below)
- refers to people's views in detail ✓

- some slips, e.g. 'are anti'
- the writer includes own view once ✗

Did YOU Know?

When *Coronation Street* first hit the TV screens in 1960, the *Daily Mirror* reviewer said, 'I find it hard to believe that viewers will want to put up with a continuous slice of domestic drudgery two evenings a week.' How wrong he was!

Spot Check

1 Which is usually written in more formal language, a discussion or a review?

2 'You shouldn't include your own opinion in a review.' True or false?

3 Give two connectives that could be useful in a discussion.

WRITING — Writing to persuade, argue, advise

Structure and planning

- When planning an argument, brainstorm a **series of points**, then put them in a **logical order**. This is a useful planning tool:

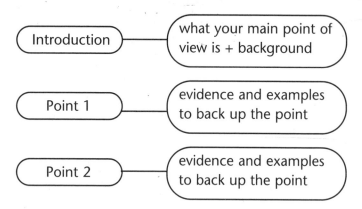

Introduction → what your main point of view is + background

Point 1 → evidence and examples to back up the point

Point 2 → evidence and examples to back up the point

Top Tip!

You can make up quotations from 'experts' to back up your arguments.

- Give each point a **new paragraph**.

- Begin with an **introduction** and end with a powerful **conclusion**.

- **Connectives** are important to join up your ideas, e.g. *therefore, because, firstly*.

Language and style

- Think about the purpose and audience of the task. If you want to sound **reasonable**, use **formal language** and avoid exaggerating.

- Think of your **opponent's arguments** and try to counter them.

- Include some **rhetorical techniques**, e.g.
  - **emotive words**: *starving* (not *hungry*), *children* (not *people*)
  - **repetition**: *it isn't fair and it isn't just*
  - **alliteration**: *a **pr**essing **pr**oblem*
  - **rhetorical questions** (where the answer is obvious): *Are we to take this seriously?*
  - **personal pronouns**: *we* includes the audience, *you* addresses the audience directly

- For **more persuasive** writing, such as a speech encouraging a sports team, include more rhetorical techniques!

- When **writing to advise**, use softer language and a friendly informal tone. Include words like *should, could, may* and *perhaps*.

Page 51 (advice texts).

Look at this level 4 argument. The version below is much more persuasive (level 5).

level
4

I think that footballers are paid the right amount of money for what they do. They are very skilful and strong and work very hard. It's a hard game so they can't play for years and years so they have to make a lot of money quickly. They give a lot of people a lot of pleasure watching them.

level
5

Footballers are definitely paid the right amount of money for what they do. You have to admit that at the top level they are skilful and strong athletes who work very hard.

Football is a tough contact sport so players have to make a lot of money quickly. They have to retire early, so what are they going to live on then?

Footballers also give a huge amount of pleasure to millions of spectators.

stronger opening ('definitely')

direct address ('you')

new point, so new paragraph

rhetorical question

more powerful language

Did YOU Know?

Many politicians have professional speech-writers to write their speeches for them.

Spot Check

1 How do paragraphs help you structure an argument?
2 Give two rhetorical techniques.
3 Which of these adjectives would you avoid in persuasive writing?
fantastic, wonderful, amazing, good, excellent

WRITING Raising your level

Follow these guidelines to improve your writing from level 4 to level 5.

Structure and organisation

- **Organise** your writing in a clear way. Include an introduction and a conclusion. Make sure any story has a beginning, a middle and an end.

- Use **paragraphs** – a new paragraph for each point, or for a change of scene, character, etc.

- Include a few **connectives** (link words) to link the ideas in your sentences.

Content

- In **stories**, make your characters interesting. Try to show what they are feeling. Include some conversation to help you do this.

- In **non-fiction**, think of your main points before you start writing.

- Develop some of your ideas, e.g. by giving examples or evidence.

Language and style

- Think about the **individual words** you use. Can you make any more interesting or effective?

- Keep the **purpose** and **viewpoint** of your writing consistent: if you are writing 'in role', keep to that role.

- Try to include some **stylistic effects**, e.g. rhetorical techniques in persuasive writing.

Top Tip!

Give yourself enough checking time – this is where you can pick up those extra marks.

Punctuation, grammar and spelling

- Use **punctuation** accurately to structure your sentences and make the meaning clear.

- Don't make any basic **grammatical** errors.

- Make sure you **spell** all simple words correctly.

Remember to practise spelling!

This is the start of a level 4 piece of writing. The task is to advise students on how to do their homework.

> You should follow this advice ...
>
> Try to follow a routine, like studying when you get home from school Routines are helpfull. so is taking a few breaks, don't works for hours on end please! And if you don't want to be disterbed don't do you're homework in the siting room with the telly on it will disterb you. I do this lot's and it doesn't work.

level 4

The improvements made here give it a level 5.
(Note: there are still some spelling errors, underlined in red.)

level 5

> ### How to study
>
> Do you want to improve your study skills? Then simply follow this advice ...
>
> • Try to follow a routine. Routines help you orginise your time. If you get into the habit of doing your homework when you get home from school, it will help.
>
> • Don't work non-stop. Regular breaks actually help you cos you return to work refreshed. You will get bored and fed up if you do your homework for hours on end.
>
> • Don't get distracted. A noisy place is a disaster if you want to do good homework effectiveley so avoid doing it on the bus, or in the television room with your mobile switched on. The interuptions will seriously distract you from doing any proper work.

Includes a title and a more effective introduction.

Each point has its own paragraph (bullet point).

Each point is developed a bit more, e.g. by giving a reason or example.

Audience and purpose is kept in mind throughout – no reference to the writer's own experience.

Language is a bit more interesting, e.g. 'distracted'.

Spelling and punctuation is more accurate (though not completely!).

Shakespeare's plays are an essential part of the Key Stage 3 (and Key Stage 4) curriculum but students often get a bit stressed about studying his work because it can seem complicated when you first start to read it. Don't panic! Your teacher and this book will see you through and not only will you understand what is happening, you'll even enjoy the play and find yourself wondering which one you'll study at Key Stage 4. This book mainly draws examples from two famous plays, *The Tempest* and *Romeo and Juliet*.

Top tips when starting Shakespeare

- Give it a go and try to read the **words aloud** – they might look strange on the page but will often make sense when you hear them.

- Try to see the play on **stage** or **screen**, or, better still, have a go yourself!

- Try to **remember** who the **characters** are. Some of the characters can have strange or unfamiliar names so draw a family tree or cut out faces for each of the characters so you can remember who says what.

- Pull out the **words** and **phrases** that you especially like – maybe make them into a poster with key images on them?

- If the plot gets complicated (and it often does) try making a **plot diagram** to keep track of what is happening.

- Try to have fun – there are often really funny bits in every play. Watch out for them!

Key areas to consider

- **Character and motivation** – who the main characters are and why they behave as they do.

  Pages 84–5.

- **Ideas, themes and issues** – the key ideas the play explores and makes you think about.

  Pages 86–7.

- **Language** – what the characters say and the impact this is intended to and does have on the audience.

  Pages 78–9, and 88–9.

- **Performance** – how the the play works on stage and how the audience responds to it. Think about how you might put on the play if you were the director.

  Pages 90–1.

Your teacher might give you a practice question like this. The
labels show you how easy it is to break down a question before
you start planning your answer.

Romeo and Juliet

Act 1 Scene 1, lines 98 to 232
Act 2 Scene 2, lines 1 to 57

**What do you learn about Romeo's character in
these extracts?**

*Support your ideas by referring to both of the extracts which are
printed on the following pages.*

18 marks

The **play** you have
been studying.
You will be given a
question that
relates to your play
only.

The **extracts** that
you have to refer to
in your answer. You
will be given a copy
of the extracts to
refer to.

The **question** that
you have to answer.

Two reminders:
- Refer to **both** of
  the extracts in
  your answer.
- **Quote** from the
  extracts.

Did You Know?

There have been over
400 films made of
Shakespeare's plays.

Director

Spot Check

True or false?
1 You are assessed on your historical knowledge about
   Shakespeare's life and times.
2 You will be asked about one Shakespeare play.
3 You should spend 10 minutes planning your answer.

Shakespeare's plays

Shakespeare wrote different kinds of plays

- **Tragedies** are serious and end with the main character's death. They explore power, jealousy, ambition and love. Example: *Romeo and Juliet*.

- **Comedies** are light-hearted and have a happy ending. They explore the relationships of men and women in love, and include misunderstandings and disguise. Example: *Much Ado About Nothing*.

- **Histories** tell the story of English kings. They explore conflict, loyalty and what it means to be a king. Example: *Richard III*.

- **Romances** begin tragically and end happily. They are sometimes called 'tragicomedies'. Example: *The Tempest*.

Shakespeare's world

William Shakespeare (born 1564, died 1616) lived during the reigns of Elizabeth I and James I. The world was very different then:

- **Kings and queens** were all-powerful. People believed they were chosen by God to rule the country.

- The **upper classes** (nobles, e.g. dukes) also had a lot of power. The **lower classes** (ordinary people) had to respect the upper classes.

- There was a lot of **political conflict**, including plots against the rulers.

- **Men** had far more power than women.

- People were very **religious** and **superstitious**. They believed in witches and magic.

> **Top Tip!**
>
> Learn about Shakespeare and his world to get a better understanding of your play – but don't write about these facts unless they are relevant to the question.

The theatre

- The theatre was very **popular** in Shakespeare's day – people had no TV or cinema. Rich and poor all watched his plays.

- **Stage** and **scenery** were very simple. There were many rough and ready outdoor productions.

- Plays are divided into **acts**. Each act has one or more **scenes**. They include dialogue and stage directions.

Example

This extract from *The Tempest* shows some key features of Shakespeare's plays.

> ### Act 1 Scene 1
>
> On a ship at sea. A tempestuous noise of thunder and lightning heard.
> *Enter a Shipmaster and a Boatswain severally*
>
> MASTER   Boatswain!
> BOATSWAIN   Here, master: what cheer?
> MASTER   Good, speak to the mariners: fall to't yarely, or we run ourselves aground: bestir, bestir.   *[Exit]*
>
> *Enter Mariners*
>
> BOATSWAIN   Heigh, my hearts! cheerly, cheerly, my hearts! yare, yare! Take in the topsail. Tend to the master's whistle.
> Blow, till thou burst thy wind, if room enough!

This is the **opening scene** of the play. The dramatic start would help to quiet the crowds.

The **setting** is given at the start of each scene.

The **character's name** is in capitals. It is followed by their **lines** (what they say).

Stage directions.
Exit = leaves the stage

Scenery, etc. was very basic, so the audience needs to be **told exactly what is happening**.

Did YOU Know?
Women were not allowed to act in Shakespeare's day, so boys played all the female roles.

Spot Check

1 What is a history play?
2 Give two differences between the theatre in Shakespeare's time and today.
3 Give one feature of Shakespeare's comedies.

Shakespeare's language

Different kinds of language

- Most of the lines are in **verse** (usually not rhymed). Each line has a regular pattern of **10 syllables**, with emphasis on every other syllable:
  Go, charge my goblins that they grind their joints

- Some passages are in **prose** (ordinary writing), especially when comic characters and the lower classes are speaking:
  What have we here? a man or a fish? dead or alive? A fish: he smells like a fish …

- **Long speeches** are often full of expression and feeling.

- Characters often speak **alternate lines** when they are arguing.

Reading the script aloud, slowly, will help you to understand it. Do not pause at the end of the lines unless there is a comma or full stop.

Expressive language

- Shakespeare uses **striking vocabulary** (choice of words):
  - to show a character's **feelings**, e.g. *To fleer and scorn at our solemnity* (Tybalt saying what he thinks Romeo intends to do, in *Romeo and Juliet*).
  - to draw a vivid **picture**, e.g. *plunged in the foaming brine* (Ariel about the shipwreck, in *The Tempest*).

- He also **plays with words**, especially in comic scenes:
  Though thou canst swim like a duck, thou art made like a goose (Stephano about Trinculo, in *The Tempest*).

- **Sound effects** such as **alliteration** (repeated sounds) add power to the poetry, e.g. *Thy tempest-tossed body* (*Romeo and Juliet*).

- **Imagery** creates word pictures in the minds of the audience:
  - **similes**: *Like a rich jewel in an Ethiope's ear* (Romeo describing Juliet in *Romeo and Juliet*)
  - **metaphors**: *My lips, two blushing pilgrims, ready stand* (Romeo in *Romeo and Juliet*)
  - **personification**: *The winds did sing it to me, and the thunder* (*The Tempest*)

Strange language

Shakespeare's language is 400 years old and very poetic. It includes:

- **old-fashioned words**, e.g. *thee/thou* (= you), *thy* (= your), *hath/hast* (= has)

- **strange word order**, e.g. *Thee of thy son, Alonso, they have bereft* (= They have taken your son away from you, Alonso.)

- **missing letters**, e.g. *'scape* = escape, *shak'd* = shaked (shook). Note that *shak'd* is pronounced as one syllable, *shaked* as two syllables.

Example

The spirit Ariel describes how he casts a spell on the drunken
Caliban and his friends (*The Tempest*, Act 4 Scene 1).
Note:
• the **similes** – he compares them first to young horses
  (colts), then to calves following the sound of the herd
• the **vivid description** of the scene.

> Then I beat my tabor*,
> At which, like unback'd* colts, they prick'd their ears,
> Advanc'd their eyelids, lifted up their noses
> As they smelt music: so I charm'd their ears
> That, calf-like, they my lowing follow'd* through
> Tooth'd briers, sharp furzes, pricking goss and thorns*,
> Which enter'd their frail shins.

*drum

*not yet ridden

*they followed my 'mooing'

*all are prickly plants

Did You Know?

Many common expressions first appeared in Shakespeare's works, including 'love letter', 'puppy dog', 'wild goose chase' and 'what the dickens'.

Spot Check

1 When does Shakespeare use prose?
2 What is alliteration?
3 What is their guilt compared to in this simile from *The Tempest*?
   their great guilt, like poison given to work a great time after, now 'gins to bite the spirits

Planning your answer

Spend the first 10 minutes planning your answer. Here is a good way to do it:

1 Make sure you understand the question

Think carefully about what the question is asking you to do. Look at these questions, for example:

> How does Caliban's language show his feelings for Prospero?

This question is about Shakespeare's **language**. The focus is on **Caliban's feelings** for Prospero, in *The Tempest*.

> What problems would the director have to solve in putting on these scenes?

This question is about **performing** the play. The focus is on **problems** in performance.

> What different impressions of Romeo do we get in these extracts?

This question is about the **character** of Romeo. The focus is on the **different sides** of his character, including **why** he behaves as he does.

Top Tip!

Your essay needs to be **balanced**, so make sure you cover **all the scenes** in your planning.

2 Re-read the extracts

- Read the extracts again, **with the question in mind**.

- **Highlight the key words** or passages that relate to the question.

3 Brainstorm ideas

- Jot down some **key words** or **ideas**, and add some **quotations** next to them. Use a spider diagram or other planning tool to help you:

What impressions do we get of Romeo in Act 1 Scene 1 and Act 2 Scene 2?

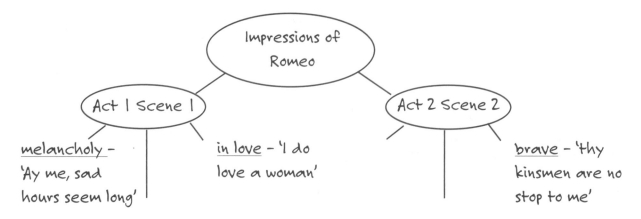

- Use this as the **plan** for your answer.

- Decide on the **order** in which you will discuss each main point.

Example

Here is a completed plan (using a different planning tool) to answer the question:

What impression do we get of Romeo in Act 1 Scene 1 and Act 2 Scene 2?

Intro	both scenes are key for R's character
Act 1 Scene 1	
melancholy	'Ay me, sad hours seem long'
in love	'I do love a woman'
in turmoil	'cold fire, sick health'
warm friend	'Good heart' (to Benvolio)
witty	'A right good mark-man!'
Act 2 Scene 2	
passionate	'It is my lady! – O, it is my love!'
romantic	'O that I were a glove upon that hand'
not proud	'My name, dear saint, is hateful to myself'
brave	'thy kinsmen are no stop to me'
reckless	'And but thou love me, let them find me here'
Conclusion	moping at first, but boldly passionate about Juliet

Did You Know?

The 'Reduced Shakespeare' theatre company have summarised all 37 of Shakespeare's plays and turned them into one fast-moving comedy lasting an hour and a half.

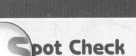 **Spot Check**

What are these questions asking you to focus on? Match each question with a focus.

Questions

1 Explain whether you think Caliban is foolish in these scenes.

2 How do Ferdinand and Miranda show in their words that they are deeply in love?

3 What advice would you give the actor playing Ariel in these scenes?

Focus of the question

a language

b performance

c character

Begin and end effectively

• Begin with an **introduction**. This should show that you **understand the question**, by referring to key words. Do not give details at this point, e.g.
Caliban shows several different feelings in these scenes.

• End with a **conclusion**. This should summarise the key points, e.g.
So we have seen that Caliban's feelings are wide-ranging. First he is …

Top Tip!

For each main point that you make in your answer, give a quotation from the extracts and explain why it is relevant (**Point – Evidence – Comment**). This shows the examiners that you are basing your ideas on the play, and that you understand the play.

Refer to the extracts

You must always refer to the extracts to back up your points. Use one of these methods for each point:

• **Summarise** the evidence in your own words, e.g.
Antonio suggests a brutal plot to murder the sleeping king.

• Include **short quotations** in your sentences. Remember to use quote marks, e.g.
In a powerful image, Ariel describes Ferdinand's hair as standing up 'like reeds'.

• Separate **longer quotations** from your text, leaving a line space before and after. Don't include more than one or two long quotations. The examiners want to see your own ideas and your own words.

Remember: **Point – Evidence – Comment**. Begin by making your own point, in your own words. Then quote from the extract to back up your point. Finally, use your own words to explain how the quotation backs up your point.

Page 83.

Write well

• **Write clearly**. Use one paragraph per point. Use words to link your ideas, e.g. *in addition, by contrast, also, however.*

• Try to **develop each point** rather than giving one straightforward fact each time.

Example

This is the beginning of an answer to the question:

How does Shakespeare make the audience laugh in Act 2 Scene 2 and Act 3 Scene 2 of *The Tempest*?

level 5

> There are all sorts of skills in these scenes to make the audience laugh. The characters are funny, there is a lot of slapstick and misunderstanding as well.
>
> To begin with Caliban thinks that Trinculo is a spirit who Prospero sends to torment him. This is funny as Trinculo is only a jester. Caliban keeps making this mistake for a long time which is funny. So after Stephano sings, Caliban says 'Do not torment me: O!' and he says it again later. Every time Caliban says this, it makes the audience laugh.

Introduction shows student understands the question and refers to the key points briefly.

Evidence is summarised in student's own words. A **comment** is still given.

Point – misunderstanding is kept going.
Evidence – 'Do not torment me: O!'
Comment – why it is effective.

One **paragraph** used for this main point.
Language is clear.

Stephano forces Caliban to drink while Trinculo hides under the covers (from Act 2 Scene 2, *The Tempest*). This photograph is from a modern interpretation performed by the Royal Shakespeare Company.

Did You Know?

You can rearrange the letters in 'William Shakespeare' to make 'I am a weakish speller'.

Spot Check

1 Explain what an introduction should do.
2 Why should you quote directly from the extracts?
3 What does the phrase 'Point – Evidence – Comment' help you to remember?

Answering questions on characters

Revising for questions on characters

You may be asked to describe how a character behaves in the set scenes. Here is how to make sure you are ready for a question like this:

- **Make a character log** for the characters in your play, with brief descriptions of who they are. Some of this could be in the form of a diagram showing connections, e.g.

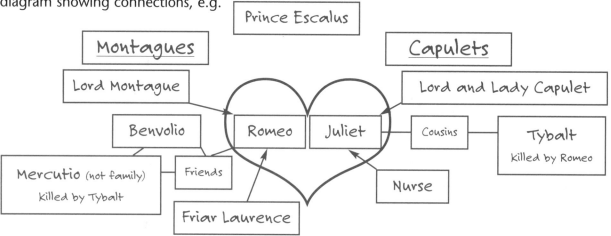

- Take two or three of the main characters and compile a **spider diagram of their key qualities**, e.g.

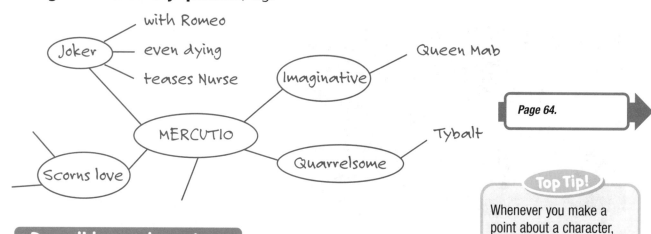

Page 64.

Top Tip!

Whenever you make a point about a character, back it up with a quotation from the extracts.

Describing a character

When describing what a character is like, refer to:

- **what they say**, e.g. *Caliban acts like a slave. He says, 'I will kiss thy foot.'*

- **what they do**, e.g. *Caliban shows Prospero 'all the qualities o' th' isle'.*

- **what others say about them**, e.g. *Trinculo calls him 'a most ridiculous monster'.*

- **why they behave as they do**, e.g. *Caliban wanted to kill Prospero so that he could live on his island as a free man.*

Did You Know?

The largest speaking part in all of Shakespeare's plays is Hamlet (nearly 1500 lines).

Writing in role

Occasionally you are asked to write as if you were one of the characters of the play. This means you have to:

- **imagine what it feels** like to be them in that situation.

- **stay in role** – refer to yourself throughout as 'I' and 'me' and keep that pretence going.

- **explain** what you are doing, thinking and feeling and why.

- **quote** from the set scenes to back up what you say.

Example

This is the start of a level 5 answer to the question:

What impression do we get of Capulet in Act 1 Scene 2 and Act 3 Scene 5 of Romeo and Juliet?

level **5**

Note the **good points**, and the **things that need improving**.

In the first scene Capulet gives the impression of being a father who worries a lot about his daughter. When Paris asks if he can marry Juliet, Capulet says, 'My child is yet a stranger in the world'. This means that she is still very young.

But Capulet is also horrible to Juliet in the second scene – he threatens to throw her out of the house when she doesn't want to marry Paris:

An you be mine, I'll give you to my friend;
And you be not, hang, beg, starve, die in the streets,
For, by my soul, I'll ne'er acknowledge thee

First paragraph uses the key word 'impression'... ✓
... but isn't really an introduction to the answer. ✗

Gives a quotation as evidence. ✓

Explains the quotation. ✓

New paragraph for a new point. ✓

Quotation given to back up point ... ✓
... but there is too much quotation and not enough explanation. ✗

Spot Check   Choose one of the main characters in your play. Draw up a spider diagram to display his or her key features or qualities.

Answering questions on ideas and themes

Knowing the story

- You won't be asked to discuss the **plot** (the story of the whole play), but you do need to know about it. Draw up a **storyline** to remind yourself, like this one about *The Tempest*:

> Act 1   The shipwreck
>
> Prospero tells Miranda about his past
>
> The history of the spirit Ariel is described
>
> Prospero and Miranda visit Caliban

Top Tip!

If you are asked about a theme, don't talk in general about it but relate it to the scenes provided. Remember to back up your ideas with quotes from the extracts.

Themes

The themes of a play are the **main ideas** it explores. You could be asked to discuss how a single theme is explored in the extracts.

The Tempest

- **forgiveness** – Prospero and his enemies, Caliban and Prospero
- **master and servant** – Caliban/Ariel and Prospero, Gonzalo and Alonso
- **magic** – Prospero a 'good' magician, Ariel a spirit
- **love and marriage** – Miranda and Ferdinand
- **parenthood** – Prospero and Miranda, Alonso and Ferdinand
- **nature v. nurture** – Prospero tries to civilise Caliban

Romeo and Juliet

- **destiny** – 'star-crossed lovers', undelivered letter
- **love and marriage** – Romeo and Juliet (and Rosaline), Paris
- **hate** – two families, Tybalt
- **parenthood** – Capulet and Juliet, Lady Capulet v. Nurse, Montague
- **death** – Mercutio, Tybalt, Romeo, Juliet, Paris, Capulet vault
- **friendship** – Romeo, Mercutio, Benvolio

Preparing for a question on theme

- Draw up a spider diagram for each theme of your play. Add detail as you study it, e.g.

Prospero a 'good' witch – uses powers to serve good

brings Ferdinand and Miranda together

arranges for a reconciliation with Antonio

Magic in 'The Tempest'

Caliban's mother Sycorax a 'bad' witch

Ariel a spirit with magic powers

Context – people believed in magic –James I wrote about witchcraft

Example

This is the start of a level 5 answer to the question:

What different ideas about love and marriage are explored in Act 3 Scene 4 and Act 3 Scene 5 of *Romeo and Juliet*?

Note the **good points**, and **the things that need improving**.

level
5

In the first scene Paris comes to woo Juliet, to win her love. Her father had intended to ask her if she would like to marry Paris, but now he assumes that she will do what she is told to do:

> ... will make a desperate tender
> Of my child's love: I think she will be ruled
> In all respects by me.

Capulet seems to want to get Juliet married off as soon as possible, as if it is a business arrangement. This is compared with the romance of the second scene.

Needs an **introduction**. ✗

First point made clearly ... ✓
... but needs backing up with quote and comment. ✗

Quotation used to back up point ... ✓
... but it isn't explained or commented on. ✗

New paragraph for a new point. ✓

Throughout the focus is on **ideas about love and marriage** in the two **scenes** given. ✓

 **Spot Check**

Draw up a spider diagram for one of the main themes of your play. Show how the theme is explored in different scenes and by different characters.

Questions on language

- You may be asked to focus on the language used in the set scenes, e.g.

  How does Caliban's language show that he is fearful …?

  How do the characters use language to battle with each other …?

  How does Shakespeare build up a mood of tension …?

- In these questions, you need to explain what the language shows, and **what effect** it has.

What the language shows

- Think about what the language is actually saying. Each sentence will have a **purpose**, which could include:
  - to persuade
  - to flatter
  - to deceive
  - to hurt
  - to fill in the background for the audience.

- When commenting on a sentence, **explain** what its purpose is, e.g.
  - *Capulet shows that he is over-confident about how well he knows Juliet when he says 'I think she will be ruled in all respects by me.'*
  - *Ariel asks, 'Was't well done?' because he is trying to gain Prospero's favour so that he can be freed.*

Top Tip!

Remember to use Point – Evidence – Comment:

Sebastian is so amazed. 'Now I will believe that there are unicorns'. ✗

Sebastian is amazed at the magic. He says, 'Now I will believe that there are unicorns' because unicorns were fabulous beasts that never existed. That shows how fabulous the sight has been. ✓

What effect the language has

- You also need to comment on **how well** the language performs its purpose. Focus on Shakespeare's **expressive language**:

Pages 78–9.

  - **imagery**, e.g. *Romeo's comparison of Juliet with 'a snowy dove trooping with crows' is appropriate because he sees her as pure and far more beautiful than other girls.*

  - **powerful words**, e.g. *Mercutio shows his disgust with Romeo's refusal to fight Tybalt by piling up the adjectives: 'O calm, dishonourable, vile submission!'*

  - **sound effects**, e.g. *Caliban almost spits his curse on Prospero (note the repeated 's' sounds): 'all the infections that the sun sucks up'.*

This is the start of a level 5 answer to the question:

Comment on the purpose and effect of these lines from Act 4
Scene 3 of *Romeo and Juliet*.

<blockquote>

Alack, alack, is it not like that I,
So early waking, what with loathsome smells,
And shrieks like mandrakes' torn out of the earth,
That living mortals, hearing them, run mad –
O, if I wake, shall I not be distraught,
Environed with all these hideous fears …

</blockquote>

level 5

Note the good points and the things that need improving.

In this speech Juliet reveals her fears about taking the sleeping potion given to her by Friar Laurence. She does this vividly, asking herself more and more questions.

These lines are effective in showing Juliet's fears about waking alone surrounded by dead bodies. They build up a picture of all the things she fears, and how they might all overwhelm her and drive her mad.

The repetition of 'Alack, alack' shows her distress and sense of helplessness. This is reinforced by the hard, harsh-sounding 'k' sounds in 'waking', 'shrieks' and 'mandrakes'. The near repetition of 'waking' and 'wake' emphasises her anxiety about the moment of waking.

The **purpose** of the language is given … ✔
… but it could add that the questions show her uncertainty and that her unfinished sentence ('… run mad –') shows her intense anxiety. ✗

The **effect** of the language is commented on … ✔
… but we need details of her fears and how they are described: the strong word 'loathsome' and the comparison with mandrakes (supposed to shriek when uprooted), and how these appeal to the senses. ✗

Effective use of **quotation** here: point – evidence – comment. ✔

Did YOU Know?

Some of Shakespeare's plays are written completely in verse, such as *King John*, *Richard II* and *Henry VI Part 1*.

Answering questions on performance

In the director's chair

The question may ask you to **imagine that you are directing** the set scenes, e.g.

> What advice would you give to the actor playing Prospero?
>
> How would you direct the scene to bring out the feeling between Romeo and Juliet?

- As a director, you need to think about these aspects of the performance:
  - most importantly, the **acting** – how the actors say their lines, move about the stage and relate to other characters
  - the **set** and **costume design**, **lighting** and **sound**.

Answering the question

- You must **explain** why you are directing in a particular way. That means understanding what the characters are doing and why, e.g.
  He should sink to the ground at this point. ✗
  He is in complete despair, so he should sink to the ground at this point. ✓

- You must **link your ideas with the text** by quoting, e.g.
  When Romeo says 'I do protest, I never injured thee' he should make an open-handed gesture towards Tybalt to show that he bears him no ill will.

> **Top Tip!**
>
> Imagine the actors on stage as they say their lines. How can movement or feeling really bring out the meaning of their words?

Focus on character and mood

- Bring out the **feelings** or **key features** of the character in your direction, e.g.
  To show his <u>anger</u> with Juliet makes him want to hit her, Capulet should raise his hand threateningly on his words 'My fingers itch'.

- **Emphasise** a particular **mood** by varying the voice, or pace, or adding pauses, e.g.
  Balthasar should <u>pause</u> after 'Then …', and then <u>sound almost pleading</u> on '… she is well, and nothing can be ill'.

Here is part of a level 5 answer to the question:

How would you direct Caliban in *The Tempest* Act 1 Scene 2 to bring out his relationship with Prospero?

Caliban should run onto the stage, hurling his curse at Prospero. He should be defiant when he says 'This island's mine'. He should point accusingly at Prospero at 'Which thou takest from me'. This will underline how angry he feels with Prospero at losing his freedom.

how Caliban should move and speak

point of direction

evidence (quoted)

comment, explaining the direction

Prospero and Caliban threaten and curse each other vehemently (Act 1 Scene 2, *The Tempest*).

Did You Know?

Shakespeare knew how to write for actors because he was an actor as well as a playwright.

Spot Check

True or false?
1 When you are asked to be a director, you have to put on a performance.
2 You don't have to describe how the scenes would have been performed in Shakespeare's day.
3 You can include thoughts on the best lighting and sound.
4 You don't have to quote from the extracts in this kind of question.

Raising your level

To raise your level from level 4 to level 5, follow these guidelines.

Show your understanding

- Show that you really understand the characters, especially **why** they are behaving as they are, e.g.
  Caliban is angry because he used to be free and now he is Prospero's slave.
  Mercutio is disgusted because Romeo refuses to fight Tybalt.

- Show that you know **how language is used to create an effect.** Comment on words and phrases that tell us what a character is feeling or thinking, or what impact Shakespeare is trying to make, e.g.
  The phrase 'great master' shows how much Ariel is a slave to Prospero.
  Capulet seems to show love for Juliet when he says 'She is the hopeful lady of my earth', but this is in contrast to the later scene in which he angrily calls her 'green-sickness carrion', 'baggage' and 'tallow-face'.

Quote effectively

- Quote from the extracts frequently, but only to **back up your points**. The quotes must be relevant to the point you are making.

Top Tip!

Only tell the story of the scene if it is relevant to the point you are making.

- Short quotations are better than long ones, e.g.
  Caliban reassures them that the noises on the island are harmless:

  > *Be not afeard: the isle is full of noises,*
  > *Sounds and sweet airs, that give delight, and hurt not.*
  > *Sometimes a thousand twangling instruments*
  > *Will hum about mine ears*

  Caliban reassures them that the noises on the island are harmless ('hurt not'). ✓

- Give a **comment** explaining why the quotation makes your point, e.g.
  Balthasar delays breaking news of Juliet's death: 'Then she is well, and nothing can be ill.' In a way this is true, because she is in heaven, but his real reason for sounding reassuring is that he cannot bear to tell Romeo something so awful.

Look at the beginning of this level 5 answer to the question:

What impression do we get of Friar Laurence in Act 2 Scene 3 and Act 4 Scene 2?

level
5

In the first scene we get the impression that Friar Laurence is a calm, philosophical man who appreciates nature, especially the 'powerful grace' of the herbs he gathers. But he is wise and knows that 'Virtue itself turns vice, being misapplied', which could apply to people as well as herbs. This makes him seem a good person to advise Romeo. His attitude towards Romeo is half-way between fatherly and friendly.

Friar Laurence often gives wise comments on life, which sometimes sounds like proverbs: '... where care lodges, sleep will never lie.' His wisdom and understanding of Romeo tell him that Romeo being awake at dawn means he is troubled 'with some distemp'rature'. He is also a man who believes in straight talking: 'Riddling confession finds but riddling shrift.' Again, this is like a proverb. The short statement sounds kind but stern.

No introduction, but answer refers immediately to the key word 'impression'.

Focus throughout is on impressions of Friar Laurence – answer shows his character is understood.

Notes how language creates an effect and adds a comment on the quotation.

Did You Know?

William Shakespeare had eleven different ways of spelling his name.

Answers to Spot Check questions

p. 7 **1** b **2** c **3** a

p. 8 **1** plot, setting, language and characters **2** when things are sorted out at the end

p. 11 **1** a narrative written as if one of the characters is telling it **2** by showing how they look, how they speak, what they do **3** accent refers to pronunciation, dialect is a regional version of speech

p. 13 **1** to sell something **2** through powerful design, emotive words **3** to draw the reader in

p. 15 **1** **a** opinion, **b** fact **2** 'bunnies' makes you think of furry little rabbits, 'slaughtered' is stronger than killed, 'in their thousands' emphasises the scale of the killing

p. 17 **1** an account of someone's life **2** true **3** past

p. 18 **1** personification **2** metaphor **3** simile

p. 21 **1** instruction **2** to engage the reader directly **3** time connectives

p. 22 **1** they show how the ideas are linked **2** when there's a new point **3** to sum up or refer back to the beginning

p. 25 **1** to give equal emphasis to both sides of the issue **2** to see whether you'd like to buy it; also to be entertained by the writing **3** a film

p. 27 **1** *Can you up your water intake …* **2** *That's wicked, man; It's really nice; It is perfectly delightful*

p. 28 **1** true **2** false **3** false

p. 30 **1** understanding what the author is suggesting rather than what is stated directly **2** false

p. 32 **1** (e.g.) to organise the passage into different points **2** (e.g.) it sets the tone straightaway

p. 41 **1** false **2** true **3** false

p. 43 **1** argue **2** instruct **3** inform/describe **4** persuade

p. 44 **1** false **2** true **3** true

p. 46 **1** (e.g.) atrocious, terrible, useless, dreadful **2** (e.g.) useless, dreadful, terrible, atrocious **3** fab

p. 49 (e.g.) Kevin took the bus to town. He didn't want to miss the start of the film, so he pushed through the crowds.

p. 50 **1** (e.g.) when there is a new place or a new character **2** false **3** a sentence that gives the main point of the paragraph

p. 53 letter: 1, 3, 5; speech: 2, 4

p. 55 **1** to begin sentences, to begin proper names **2** Graeme's mobile rang. It was Paula calling from Oxford. **3** 'It's endless, isn't it?' she said, looking at the minutes go by.

p. 57 **1** He used the colours red, white, yellow and blue. **2** Lucy, the youngest of the children, is really the most important character. **3** Stuart was replaced at half-time, which was the final straw.

p. 59 **1** flys (flies), gasses (gases) **2** skating – skated, skidding – skidded, respecting – respected **3** found, stole, travelled, bought

p. 61 **1** queitly (quietly), dissappoint (disappoint), wierd (weird), ocasion (occasion) **2** 'their' means belonging to them, 'there' means over there

p. 63 **1** Beginning, middle, end **2** false **3** keep it short, make it realistic

p. 65 **1** (e.g.) it helps you brainstorm ideas **2** they are describing words **3** a way of making the reader picture something, especially by using a simile or metaphor

p. 67 **1** false **2** because the explanation itself should be written one step at a time **3** (e.g.) because, then, first

p. 69 **1** discussion **2** false **3** (e.g.) however, on the other hand

p. 71 **1** you give each point of your argument a new paragraph **2** (e.g.) repetition, emotive words **3** good

p. 75 **1** false **2** true **3** true

p. 77 **1** a play based on history and focused on a king of England **2** (e.g.) theatre was more popular then, and plays were performed during the day (in the light) **3** (e.g.) there is a happy ending

p. 79 **1** for the lower class characters **2** when words begin with similar sounds **3** to poison

p. 81 **1** c **2** a **3** b

p. 83 **1** refer to key words in the question to show you understand it **2** to show that you are basing your ideas on the play, and that you understand the play **3** how to use evidence from the extracts: make your own point, then quote from the extract to back it up, then explain how the quote does this

p. 91 **1** false **2** true **3** true **4** false

Glossary

adjective   a describing word, e.g. 'red', 'evil'

advice   a text type which has the aim of suggesting a course of action

alliteration   the effect created when words next to each other begin with the same letter (e.g. 'terrible twins')

analyse   to investigate something carefully and thoroughly

apostrophe   a punctuation mark used to show either possession (e.g. 'Dave's computer') or a missing letter (e.g. 'can't')

argument   a text type which presents and develops a particular point of view

audience   someone who listens to or reads a text

bias   weighting a text unfairly in favour of one side or the other

blank verse   in Shakespeare's plays, unrhymed verse with 10 syllables in each line

characterisation   how an author presents and develops their characters

clause   a group of words in a sentence which expresses a single idea; a clause has a verb and usually a subject

colon   a punctuation mark that introduces a clause which leads on from or explains another clause

comedy   a Shakespearean play about relationships with a happy ending

command   a verb that gives an instruction to the reader, e.g. 'Think about your children …'

complex sentence   a sentence with one main clause and one or more subordinate clauses

compound sentence   a sentence made up of two or more simple sentences linked by 'and', 'but' or 'or'

connective   a word or phrase which links clauses and sentences, to signal to the audience where the text is going

direct address   using the second person ('you') to hold the reader's attention in a text

discussion   a text type which helps the audience understand an issue by presenting the different viewpoints fairly

emotive language   words, phrases and ideas designed to make the audience feel something strongly

explanation   a text type which helps the audience understand why or how something is as it is

fact   a piece of knowledge or information that can be proved to be true

fiction   anything that is made up, especially a story

formal language   writing or speech that follows the strictest rules of Standard English

homophone   a word that sounds the same as another but is spelt differently, e.g. 'where' and 'wear'

imagery   the use of language to create an image or picture; *see also* simile, metaphor, personification

informal language   language that does not follow the strict rules of Standard English

information   a text type which presents facts in a way that is easy to understand

instruction   a text type which tells the audience how to do something, through a series of sequenced steps

inverted comma   a punctuation mark used to show the beginning and end of direct speech

media   the term given to texts aimed at large numbers of people, e.g. television, magazines, newspapers, Internet

metaphor   a type of imagery which describes something as something else, e.g. 'you are an island'

motivation   why a character behaves as he or she does

non-fiction   any text that is not made up

opinion   a person's own view about something

paragraph   a group of sentences on one topic, person or event. A new paragraph begins a new line.

paraphrase   to summarise part of the text in your own words

person   a way of referring to pronouns and verbs according to whether they indicate the speaker/writer (1st person: 'I', 'we'), the audience (2nd person: 'you') or someone else (3rd person: 's/he', 'it', 'they')

personification   a type of imagery which refers to objects as if they were human, e.g. 'the sun punished them'

persuasion   a text type which has the aim of selling an idea or a product

phrase   a group of words which go together, e.g. 'the garden gate'

plot   the storyline

popular newspaper   a newspaper that aims to entertain as much as to inform its readers, e.g. *The Sun, The Mirror*

prefix   letters added at the start of a word to change its meaning

punctuation   a way of marking text with symbols to make the meaning clear

purpose   the aim of a text

recount   a text type which tells the reader what happened, often in an informative and entertaining way

relative clause   part of the sentence beginning 'who', 'which', 'that' etc. which gives more information about the main clause

rhetorical question   a question asked for effect, not for an answer

rhetorical technique   a technique used to persuade an audience, e.g. emotive language, sound effects, repetition, rhetorical questions

romance   a Shakespearean play that mixes elements of tragedy and comedy

scan   to look over a text quickly in order to find a particular word or piece of information

semi-colon   a punctuation mark used to show a pause in a sentence longer than a comma

simile   a type of imagery which compares something with something else, making the comparison clear by using a phrase such as 'like; or 'as if', e.g. 'she swam like a fish'

simple sentence   a sentences with only one clause

skim   to read a whole text quickly

slogan   a memorable phrase used to sell a product

Standard English   the type of spoken and written English that is generally considered 'correct' and that is taught in schools

suffix   letters added at the end of a word to change its meaning

summarise   to identify the key points of a text

text   a block of spoken or written language

theme   the underlying ideas or issues that a story or play deals with

tone   a measure of the quality, mood or style of a piece of writing

topic sentence   the main sentence in a paragraph, which gives the topic (subject) of the paragraph

tragedy   a Shakespearean play with an unhappy ending

verb   a word that refers to an action, e.g. 'runs' or a state of being, e.g. 'feels'

Index

Collins Revision

KS3 English Workbook

Lucy English

Reading skills

When we think of reading we tend to just think of being able to understand the words and the story. However, there's more to being a great reader than that!

Being a great reader means you are able to pick out specific words and phrases from the text to act as evidence for your ideas. You are also able to look beyond surface meaning and make **deductions** and **interpret information**. Great readers can also work out and explain how a text works – this means looking at the **structure** and **organisation** such as the layout or how the writing develops. The language of the text is something students often find difficult to write about, but a great reader is able to do just that and explain how a word or phrase creates a particular meaning. Finally, great readers are able to identify and comment on why a text has been written and what the author intended it to do.

All of these features of a great reader have been broken down into different Assessment Focuses for KS3 and you will encounter them during your English lessons and in your Teacher Assessment at the end of Year 9.

Reading Assessment Focuses

AF1: use a range of strategies, including accurate decoding of text, to read for meaning.

This means you are able to read beyond the surface meaning of the text and can work out any connotations and implications.

AF2: understand, describe, select or retrieve information, events or ideas from texts and use quotation and reference to text

This means you need to show you understand what you have read by picking ideas and evidence out of the text. You can also put events and ideas in your own words.

AF3: deduce, infer or interpret information, events or ideas from texts

This means you can make links between ideas. You read between the lines and work out the story or idea that is implied.

AF4: identify and comment on the structure and organisation of texts, including grammatical and presentational features at text level

This means you can explain how and why the text is structured in the way it is. This might refer to layout or how the writing develops.

AF5: explain and comment on writers' use of language, including grammatical and literary features at word and sentence level

This means you can write about the language of the text and explain why certain words or phrases have been used and the effect they have on the reader.

AF6: identify and comment on writers' purposes and viewpoints and the overall effect of the text on the reader

This means you can look at the big picture – you can explain why the writer has written the text and what they were trying to do. You can also explain what impact the whole text has on the reader.

The texts

This part of your KS3 English pack contains ten practice reading texts for you to work through. Each text has a series of questions that test your reading skills. These questions all test a different Assessment Focus, just as in your English lessons and in your final Teacher Assessment.

It doesn't matter how long you spend on these tasks – in fact, it's better to take the time you need to make sure your answers are brilliant! To check your answers, turn to the back of the book.

The first thing you will need to do when you read each text is to work out the **purpose**, **audience** and **text type**. This will help you with the questions that follow. It's really good to get into the habit of using this skill whenever you are reading or writing as it will help ensure you are great at both.

Good luck!

1

Read the extract and answer the questions that follow.

This is the opening of a book called *Raven's Gate,* by Anthony Horowitz.

Matt Freeman knew he was making a mistake.

He was sitting on a low wall outside Ipswich station, wearing a grey hooded sweatshirt, shapeless, faded jeans, and trainers with frayed laces. It was six o'clock in the evening and the London train had just pulled in. Behind him, commuters were fighting their way out of the station. The concourse was a tangle of cars, taxis and pedestrians, all of them trying to find their way home. A traffic light blinked from red to green but nothing moved. Somebody leant on their horn and the noise blared out, cutting through the damp evening air. Matt heard it and looked up briefly. But the crowd meant nothing to him. He wasn't part of it. He never had been – and he sometimes thought he never would be.

IPSWICH

• Purpose = To describe a setting of a character
• Audience = A teenage reading texts.
• Text type = Fiction writing.

Getting to grips with the text

1 Matt is made to seem an outsider. Find one quotation that shows he does not fit in.

'He wasn't part of it, 'the crowd meant nothing to him.'

1 mark

✱ **2** How does the structure of the extract emphasise Matt's isolation?

_____

_____

_____

_____

2 marks

3 The table below gives examples of descriptive language used in the text.
Complete the table to explain the impression each word or phrase gives.

Example of descriptive language	The impression it gives
'commuters were fighting their way out of the station'	This gives the impression of pressure and chaos.
'a tangle of cars, taxis and pedestrians'	Everybody are busy & crowded.
'Somebody leant on their horn and the noise blared out'	The noise was really loud & annoying.

2 marks

4 The extract emphasises Matt's feeling of isolation and not belonging.
Explain how the whole extract creates this impression.
Support your ideas with quotations from the extract.

_____

_____

_____

_____

_____

_____

_____

_____

_____

3 marks

5 What sort of thing do you think might happen next? Provide evidence for
your answer.

Matt will get into a fight
and end up in hospital
unconsion. and feel upset about
the fight I will be upset
for ever.

_____

_____

2 marks

HW

2

Read the extract and answer the questions that follow.

> This is from a book called *The Boy in the Striped Pyjamas*, by John Boyne. It is about a nine-year-old boy called Bruno.
>
> Bruno narrowed his eyes and wished he were taller, stronger and eight years older. A ball of anger exploded inside him and made him wish that he had the courage to say exactly what he wanted to say. It was one thing, he decided, to be told what to do by Mother and Father – that was perfectly reasonable and to be expected – but it was another thing entirely to be told what to do by someone else. Even by someone with a fancy title like 'Lieutenant'.

- Purpose = *Entertain, describe.*
- Audience = *Teenages & Adult*
- Text type = *Fiction writing*

1 Why is Bruno angry?

He is angry because we wish something and wish to be taller and strong.

1 mark

2 The writer describes the way Bruno is feeling very clearly. Identify two words or phrases that show his anger.

A ball of anger exploded inside.

1 mark

3 Complete the table, explaining what each of these quotations tells us about Bruno's state of mind.

Quotation	What it tells us about Bruno's state of mind
'Bruno narrowed his eyes and wished he were taller, stronger and eight years older'	*Angry mood and confussed to be a young person.*
'A ball of anger exploded inside him'	*His face goes red.*

2 marks

4 What is Bruno's attitude towards the Lieutenant? Provide a quotation to support your answer.

'A ball of anger explode inside him'

5 Bruno refers to his parents as 'Mother' and 'Father'. Why does this make him seem young?

The reason why is because older people say parents.

6 The writer makes us take Bruno's side in this extract. How has he done this?

The writer made people on their side because they made Bruno a little child and described him as he was cute.

3

Read the extract and answer the questions that follow.

Young people can take centre stage this summer with Woking Borough Council's arts workshops.

SUMMER FUN IN JULY AND AUGUST

Calling all budding actors and artists! There is a packed programme of activities lined up this summer to get your creative juices really flowing.

If you fancy yourself as an actor, why not join one of the **drama workshops** at the Rhonda McGaw theatre? These will give you a chance to develop your theatre skills while exploring some exciting scripts from top writers including Salman Rushdie and Timberlake Wertenbaker.

You'll have lots of fun learning new skills and meeting other young people with a flair for the stage. And you can show off your talents when you invite family and friends to a final performance at the end of the week.

Or if you'd like to see behind the screen at the Rhoda McGaw theatre, you can sign up for a **cinema crafts workshop** in August. You'll be able to make your own costumes and props for the show for the afternoon film. The workshops are suitable for children aged 7–11, and discounts for Passport to Leisure holders are available.

Crafty types aged between 7 and 11 can make their mark at **arts workshops** at Woking Youth Arts Centre, Knaphill, on 27th or 28th July. Try African drumming or make your own Mexican crafts at a Holiday Fiesta workshop – and take your creations home at the end of the day.

The Craft Co. will also be running workshops for children aged 6 and above at The Barn in Worplesdon throughout August. There's a huge range of activities available, including T-shirt painting, salt-dough modelling, card-making and pot-decorating.

Young dancers and poets aged between 8 and 16 have their chance to shine between 22nd and 26th August at Woking College Dance Studio.

Working with professional dancers, you can contribute your ideas to a new words and movement experience. Friends and family are welcome to watch the final performance on Friday afternoon.

- Purpose = _Entertainment._
- Audience = _7 to 18 years old and maybe their parent_
- Text type = _Magazine article_

Getting to grips with the text

1 This article outlines summer activities for young people in Woking. Give one activity that will be available and some details of what it will include.

Drama workshops = this will give children a chance to develope the threater.

2 marks

2 The language used makes the opportunities sound exciting.
Complete the table to explain what the language suggests in each example.

Example of language used	What it suggests
'a packed programme'	The alliteration makes it sound fun and exciting.
'a huge range of activities'	
'chance to shine'	

2 marks

3 How does the whole article make the opportunities available for young people in Woking during the summer seem exciting and attractive?
You should comment on how the extract:
• Makes the activities seem exciting and fun
• Makes it seem easy to join, even if you don't know anyone
• Uses presentation and layout devices to help the reader find the information they might be interested in.

For young people to work during the summer while make a progess in school and also it will be a good thing for them

5 marks

Read the letter and answer the questions that follow.

LeisureTime Plus
Rock Hill Road
Sheffield
01234 567890

Dear Ms Holroyd,

Everybody knows the need to live a healthy lifestyle but did you know that regular exercise can boost your immune system and improve your energy levels by up to 50%? Experts have shown that people who exercise for just 30 minutes three times a week are fitter, healthier and happier. At LeisureTime Plus we want to help you reach this state.

Forget all you might think about crowded, sweaty gyms and sergeant-major fitness instructors with the bark of a bulldog; our staff and facilities are second to none and help to make exercise fun and rewarding. We're not saying it's going to be a walk in the park, but we'll be with you all the way as you travel your journey to a fitter, happier you.

Just think, in four weeks you'll notice your skin will have a new, radiant glow, in six weeks your jeans will be easier to do up, and in twelve weeks you'll be running up flights of stairs without a thought. Sound good? Well just sign up for our fabulous new introductory offer today and this could be your reality.

Call LeisureTime Plus today for more details, we're looking forward to helping find the new you.

Yours truly,

Malcolm Day

Director, LeisureTime Plus

- Purpose = <u>Not entertainment for childrens</u>
- Audience = <u>Adults & elderlys.</u>
- Text type = <u>formal letter.</u>

> **Getting to grips with the text**

1 What does this letter want the reader to do?

<u>To make a easy life style.</u>

1 mark

2 The letter is addressed to a specific person, Ms Holroyd. What sort of person does the letter suggest Ms Holroyd is?

<u>The sort of person Ms Holroyd would be is a elderly.</u>

2 marks

3 Explain two different ways in which the letter makes exercise sound appealing.

- _putting different fun activitys_
- _making it feel fun._

2 marks

4 The letter uses negative phrases to describe bad fitness experiences.
Fill in the table to explain why the language is used in this way.

Example of negative phrase	Why the language is used in this way
'crowded, sweaty gyms'	
'sergeant-major fitness instructors with the bark of a bulldog'	

2 marks

5 The letter uses informal, colloquial phrases. Identify one of these phrases and explain why it is used.

- Informal, colloquial phrase: _you'll notice your skin_
- Why it is used: _to preusdived them._

2 marks

6 Explain how this letter makes joining LeisureTime Plus seem a good idea.
In your answer you should write about:
- The use of fact and opinion
- The tone of the letter
- The use of language.

It's a good idea because it has magic work to inspire people.
The use of language make them fun and the tone of the letter of is it formal to public people.

5 marks

5

Read the newspaper article and answer the questions that follow.

SCHOOLKIDS TO BE GIVEN MOBILE PHONES
Government heralds a huge step forward in learning technology

Government ministers were celebrating yesterday after announcing a deal with mobile phone manufacturers to give these gadgets to all schoolchildren. They are confident the newest range of phones will help students learn in today's techno-world.

Wayne Daniels, advisor for education, said this move would enable children to interact with lessons in a modern way as they could be used as personal organisers and even record parts of lessons. "Students won't be able to claim they forgot to do their homework," he said, "not when it's recorded onto the phone's organiser with an alarm set for that evening."

Backers of this scheme reel off lists of benefits: students will be able to use the organiser, the memo facility, research using the Internet, share ideas in class, manipulate sounds in music; there's even the alarm to get them up in the morning and prevent them being late for school!

However, teachers are questioning this move, claiming that phones are a nuisance, constantly interrupting lessons and providing a target for bullies and thieves. They demand to know how much money has been spent on this project, and suggest some of this could have been spent improving the many dilapidated school buildings around the country.

Students, meanwhile, were celebrating!

Getting to grips with the text

- Purpose = _____
- Audience = _Teenagers_
- Text type = _Newsletter ._

1 Identify two ways that it is claimed mobile phones will help students' learning.

- _Make then have a break_
- _If they forget their calculation they can go on their Phone._

1 mark

2 How does the writer show that the teachers' views are going to be different from the views already described in the article?

By them It's going to change their idea

3 What does the phrase 'today's techno-world' suggest?

It Suggest

4 What is the effect of having a quotation from the education advisor?

5 Some of the language used in the paragraph about the teachers' response is very negative. Pick two negative words or phrases and explain the impression they create.

• _____

_____

_____

• _____

_____

_____

6 Does this article present all views in a balanced way? Use evidence to support your ideas.

_____

_____

_____

_____

_____

_____

_____

_____

_____

_____

_____

_____

Read the poem and answer the questions that follow.

Blackberry picking
(for Philip Hobsbaum)
by Seamus Heaney

Late August, given heavy rain and sun
For a full week, the blackberries would ripen.
At first, just one, a glossy purple clot
Among others, red, green, hard as a knot.
You ate that first one and its flesh was sweet
Like thickened wine: summer's blood was in it
Leaving stains upon the tongue and lust for
Picking. Then red ones inked up and that hunger
Sent us out with milk-cans, pea-tins, jam-pots
Where briars scratched and wet grass bleached our boots.
Round hayfields, cornfields and potato-drills
We trekked and picked until the cans were full,
Until the tinkling bottom had been covered
With green ones, and on top big blobs burned
Like a plate of eyes. Our hands were peppered
With thorn pricks, our palms sticky as Bluebeard's.

We hoarded the fresh berries in the byre.
But when the bath was filled we found a fur,
A rat-grey fungus, glutting on our cache.
The juice was stinking too. Once off the bush
The fruit fermented, the sweet flesh would turn sour.
I always felt like crying. It wasn't fair
That all the lovely canfuls smelt of rot.
Each year I hoped they'd keep, knew they would not.

Bluebeard was a savage murderer who killed his first six wives.
briars = the long, thorny stems that blackberries grow on
cache = a collection, store or treasure

• Purpose = _____
• Audience = _____
• Text type = _____

Getting to grips with the text

1 The poem describes blackberry picking. Every year the narrator tries to pick and keep blackberries but isn't able to. What happens?

_____

2 The narrator says they collected the blackberries in 'milk-cans, pea-tins, jam-pots'. What does this suggest about the blackberry collectors?

_____

1 mark

3 What is the impact of the final line?

_____

1 mark

4 Find and write down an example of a simile. Explain why the poet has used this image.

Simile: _____

1 mark

Explanation: _____

_____

2 marks

_____

5 The blackberry pickers work hard to collect their fruit. What impression do you get of them? Use quotations as evidence for your ideas.

_____

_____

_____

_____

_____

_____

_____

5 marks

_____

6 The poet wrote this poem as an adult, looking back on a childhood memory. What impression does he give us of this memory?

_____

_____

_____

_____

_____

_____

_____

_____

5 marks

_____

7

Read the extract and answer the questions that follow.

How to make the scrummiest pizza

You will need:
- Plain pizza bases – you can make these using the recipe on page 12 or buy them from the supermarket
- Tomato topping – see page 14 for our tasty topping
- Mozzarella – sliced
- Your fave toppings – slice these up and put them in bowls ready to use.

These are our fave toppings:
- Ham, mushroom and sweetcorn
- Pepperoni, green peppers, mushrooms and more pepperoni
- BBQ chicken (you can get this ready cooked from the supermarket), ham and pepper
- Cheese and tomato (sometimes simple is best!)
- Prawns and spinach (honestly!)
- Peppers, mushrooms and pineapple

How to do it:

1 First, take your pizza base and plaster it with the tomato topping. Don't let this go over the edge as it'll slide off and burn in the oven!

2 Next place slices of mozzarella on the tomato – it's up to you how much you like.

3 Now for the fun bit: carefully position your favourite toppings on your pizza. There are no rules but we've found it's best to have between 2 and 5 different toppings.

4 When you are happy with your creation, carefully put it in a hot oven (180–200°C) for 12–20 minutes, depending on the size of the pizza and the amount of topping you have. It's probably best to set the timer to check it after 10 minutes. It's also a good idea to ask an adult to help with this bit.

5 You'll know when it's ready to enjoy because the cheese will have melted and it'll look and smell mouth-watering! Take it out of the oven carefully (get someone to help with this), put it on a plate and enjoy!

Don't forget the boring washing-up bit – it's worth it if you want to use the kitchen again!

- Purpose = _____
- Audience = _____
- Text type = _____

Getting to grips with the text

1 Put numbers in the boxes to show the correct order to do these things:

Put the mozzarella on the pizza	☐	Put your favourite toppings on the pizza	☐
Make the tomato topping	☐	Put the pizza in the oven	☐

1 mark

2 Who is the intended audience of this text? Explain how you know.

_____

_____

_____

3 marks

3 The language of this text helps to make it clear and easy to follow. Choose a word or phrase that is used to make it easy to follow and explain how it does this.

_____

_____

_____

3 marks

4 This text uses informal language and phrases. Identify an informal word or phrase and explain why it has been used.

_____

_____

_____

2 marks

5 In the list of 'our fave toppings' there are comments in brackets. Explain why it says '(sometimes simple is best!)' after 'Cheese and tomato'.

_____

_____

2 marks

6 Do you think this text is likely to make young people want to make the pizza? You should comment on how the text:
- Makes the recipe seem fun
- Makes a connection with the reader
- Makes the recipe seem easy.

_____

_____

_____

_____

_____

_____

_____

_____

_____

_____

_____

5 marks

8

Read the extract from *An Arrest*, by Ambrose Bierce, and answer the questions that follow on pages 116–117.

Having murdered his brother-in-law, Orrin Brower of Kentucky was a fugitive from justice. From the county jail where he had been confined to await his trial he had escaped by knocking down his jailer with an iron bar, robbing him of his keys and, opening the outer door, walking out into the night. The jailer being unarmed, Brower got no weapon with which to defend his recovered liberty. As soon as he was out of the town he had the folly to enter a forest; this was many years ago, when that region was wilder than it is now.

The night was pretty dark, with neither moon nor stars visible, and as Brower had never dwelt thereabout, and knew nothing of the lay of the land, he was, naturally, not long in losing himself. He could not have said if he were getting farther away from the town or going back to it – a most important matter to Orrin Brower. He knew that in either case a posse of citizens with a pack of bloodhounds would soon be on his track and his chance of escape was very slender; but he did not wish to assist in his own pursuit. Even an added hour of freedom was worth having.

Suddenly he emerged from the forest into an old road, and there before him saw, indistinctly, the figure of a man, motionless in the gloom. It was too late to retreat: the fugitive felt that at the first movement back toward the wood he would be, as he afterward explained, "filled with buckshot". So the two stood there like trees, Brower nearly suffocated by the activity of his own heart; the other – the emotions of the other are not recorded.

A moment later – it may have been an hour – the moon sailed into a patch of unclouded sky and the hunted man saw that visible embodiment of Law lift an arm and point significantly toward and beyond him. He understood. Turning his back to his captor, he walked submissively away in the direction indicated, looking to neither the right nor the left; hardly daring to breathe, his head and back actually aching with a prophecy of buckshot.

Brower was as courageous a criminal as ever lived to be hanged; that was shown by the conditions of awful personal peril in which he had coolly killed his brother-in-law. It is needless to relate them here; they came out at his trial, and the revelation of his calmness

in confronting them came near to saving his neck. But what would you have? – when a brave man is beaten, he submits.

So they pursued their journey jailward along the old road through the woods. Only once did Brower venture a turn of the head: just once, when he was in deep shadow and he knew that the other was in moonlight, he looked backward. His captor was Burton Duff, the jailer, as white as death and bearing upon his brow the livid mark of the iron bar. Orrin Brower had no further curiosity.

Eventually they entered the town, which was all alight, but deserted; only the women and children remained, and they were off the streets. Straight toward the jail the criminal held his way. Straight up to the main entrance he walked, laid his hand upon the knob of the heavy iron door, pushed it open without command, entered and found himself in the presence of a half-dozen armed men. Then he turned. Nobody else entered.

On a table in the corridor lay the dead body of Burton Duff.

• Purpose = _____

• Audience = _____

• Text type = _____

1 Why is Orrin Brower a 'fugitive from justice'?

_____

_____

2 What is the name of the jailer?

_____

3 The table gives examples of descriptive words and phrases used in the text.
Fill in the table to explain the impression each word or phrase gives.

Example of descriptive phrase	Impression it creates
'the moon sailed into a patch of unclouded sky'	The moon is free and moves easily. This contrasts with the actions of the fugitive.
'as white as death'	
'the livid mark of the iron bar'	

4 The first sentence of the story gives us lots of background information.

a Explain what it tells us.

_____

_____

b Explain why it includes so much information in one sentence.

_____

_____

5 The story includes hints that the man who is making Orrin return to the jail is a ghost. Identify one of these hints and explain why it is used.

_____

_____

_____

_____

6 Look again at the last two paragraphs. How does the structure of the piece make the ending dramatic?

_____

_____

_____

_____

_____

_____

_____

_____

_____

_____

_____

_____

_____

_____

_____

_____

_____

5 marks

9

Read the extract and answer the questions that follow.

★★★★★

Another cracking adventure with Wallace and Gromit

It's hard to believe it's been ten long years since Wallace last put the poor long-suffering Gromit through his paces, but now they're back, and with more gadgets than ever before! Yes, Wallace and Gromit hit the big screen, big time in a big full-length movie guaranteed to delight movie-goers of all ages.

From the moment the cheese-loving Wallace reappears on our screens, it's clear that Nick Park and his fellow animators haven't lost their touch, or their sense of humour. This film is not only a great story, but is also littered with jokes, from the 'Smug' fridge to the Austin Powers-type double entendres about melons.

The Plasticine models are a joy to see, full of fingerprints and energy in a way Computer Generated Imagery can never be. Furthermore, the voices are perfect for their characters; I even forgot superstars such as Helena Bonham-Carter and Ralph Fiennes were 'playing' Lady Tottington and Victor Quartermaine. Maybe that means they weren't really needed?

The plot isn't always as fast-moving as it could be, perhaps that's so they can make it the full-length film this is, but it's a hugely satisfying watch and justly deserving of its Oscar.

Getting to grips with the text

- Purpose = _____

- Audience = _____

- Text type = _____

1 This extract was written to review the film and express the reviewer's opinion. Explain why the stars have been put at the top of the review.

_____

1 mark

2 The review uses lots of adjectives. Identify a phrase using adjectives and explain what effect their use has.

_____

_____

1 mark

3 What technique has the reviewer used here, and what impact does it have?

'Yes, Wallace and Gromit hit the big screen, big time in a big full-length movie guaranteed to delight movie-goers of all ages.'

_____

_____

_____

2 marks

4 This is a review, so it is giving the writer's opinion. However, it does contain some facts. Identify a fact and explain why it has been used.

_____

_____

_____

2 marks

5 The review uses a friendly and informal tone. Identify a word or phrase that is friendly and informal and explain why it has been used.

_____

_____

_____

2 marks

6 The review ends with 'it's a hugely satisfying watch and justly deserving of its Oscar'. Explain how the whole of the review supports this opinion.

_____

_____

_____

_____

_____

_____

_____

_____

_____

_____

_____

_____

_____

_____

_____

5 marks

10

Read the extract and answer the questions that follow.

BORDONDOWN SCHOOL
LONGFIELD ROAD
BATH

Dear Parent

Thank you for your interest in our school. I am pleased to enclose a school prospectus and invitation to our next open day.

As you know Bordondown is a thriving school where staff and students work hard for top results. We are lucky to have some very talented members of the school community and we are looking forward to another year of excellent examination results, with many of our students going on to Oxbridge and other top universities.

The focus of every school day is learning, and every activity is geared to support your child in their journey to become a successful learner; perhaps he or she will be one of our Oxbridge students of the future?

Learning is the key to a successful life, and we insist on discipline in order to achieve it. From correct uniform to homework being completed on time, we find an organised student is a successful student.

In addition to the timetabled day, there are many extra-curricular activities available for your child; a browse through the booklet in the prospectus will outline some of these.

Although the prospectus provides a comprehensive guide to our school, the best way to find out about its workings is to visit us. We would be delighted to show you round the school, provide students for you to talk to, and answer any questions you might have. These tours do get very busy, so please book a place by returning the form or telephoning the office.

I look forward to meeting you soon,

Yours faithfully,

Matthew Best

Head teacher

Oxbridge: Oxford and Cambridge Universities

• Purpose = _____

• Audience = _____

• Text type = _____

Getting to grips with the text

1 Why has the head teacher written this letter?

_____

2 Mr Best writes about the success some students have had:
'many of our students going on to Oxbridge and other top universities.'
What does this suggest he regards as school success?

_____

_____

_____

3 Although this letter is from one person, he uses the plural pronoun 'we'
throughout. Suggest why he does this and what impression he is trying
to give.

_____

_____

_____

4 The letter uses very short paragraphs. Explain why.

_____

_____

5 What impression of Bordondown School is created by this letter?

_____

_____

_____

_____

_____

_____

_____

_____

_____

_____

_____

_____

_____

_____

_____

Practice reading paper

Try this practice reading paper.

Make sure you are in a quiet place and can spend 1 hour 15 minutes without being disturbed.

You are allowed 15 minutes reading time in the test, so set a timer or ask someone to tell you when the reading time is up.

- Spend 15 minutes reading pages 123–129 and highlighting or marking the purpose, audience and text type of each text. You might also like to mark any interesting style or language features.

- When the 15 minutes reading time is up, you can turn to the question paper. You have 1 hour to answer the questions.

- There are 14 questions about these texts and they are worth 32 marks in total.

- Remember to look at the marks available and make sure you provide enough information to get full marks.

Blood

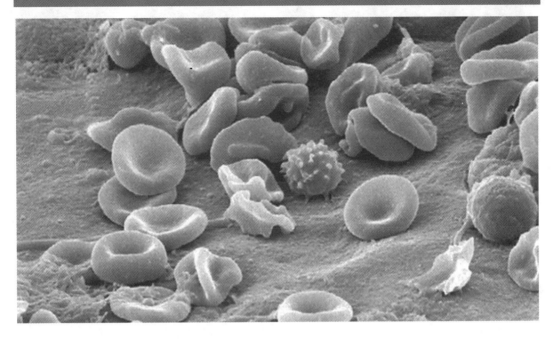

Contents

The texts in this booklet are all about blood. They explain the scientific facts about blood, and what it can tell us about people.

This is an extract from a booklet written for people who give blood. It gives information about the different colours blood can be and explains what this says about the donor.

Shades of red

What does the colour of your blood say about you?

Have you ever wondered why your blood seems to be a different shade of red from the donor on the next bed? Have you been concerned your blood looks more like Ribena than the finest Merlot? Although all blood is red, the shades vary between donors and can even be used to indicate health issues.

O n average there are 35 trillion red blood cells, suspended in plasma, circulating in your body at any one time. Red cells are filled with haemoglobin that gives your blood its red colour.

Blood naturally changes colour during its journey around your body. When you take a breath, the inhaled oxygen in your lungs attaches itself to haemoglobin in the red cells. At this point your blood is oxygenated and a strong, bright poppy-red.

On their journey around your body, red cells exchange oxygen for carbon dioxide which returns to

Our scientific staff have developed methods of visually checking the colour of your donation, as an additional safety measure. Much like a decorator's colour chart, donations are compared to a set of standard colour shades. Using colourmetric standards is another way we can help provide safer blood to the patient.

your lungs through your veins. The carbon dioxide is exhaled and the whole process begins again. At the end of the journey, your blood will appear a darker shade of red.

Blood is the transport system of your body. It not only carries energy to the cells but it also carries anything else that you ingest or absorb through your skin. Which also helps to explain why not everyone's blood is the same shade.

Having bright red blood is not necessarily a sign of good health. Heavy smokers may produce a vividly coloured donation because carbon monoxide in cigarette smoke is attached much more easily to red cells than oxygen. The blood is bright red because of the presence of a cherry-red compound called carboxyhaemoglobin, which forms when carbon monoxide binds to haemoglobin.

If blood looks pinkish, it may be due to a high level of water insoluble fats, called lipaemia. Lipaemia can be inherited or caused by a fatty diet.

Wine buffs may like to know that claret-coloured blood suggests haemoglobin may be leaking from the red cells; a natural part of blood's ageing process called haemolysis.

Colour match

You might be surprised to know our staff back at the centres look out for darker donations because deep shades imply possible bacterial contamination or incorrect storage. They are also vigilant for blood which appears to be clumped or

clotted or which looks darker in patches and may be unsuitable for transfusion.

The colour of plasma, which is usually straw-yellow, also varies enormously. Its colour can be seen after the blood has been separated, and the red cells removed. Some oral contraceptives turn plasma bright green and self-tanning pills may make it go a fluorescent orange!

Plasma is usually a clear yellow. However, it can look cloudy occasionally. This can be caused by a number of things. You could simply have eaten some fatty food before giving blood, or it could be caused by an underlying condition related to a high fat content in the body. It may even indicate a problem with the donation in relation to bacteria.

Our staff are trained to notice these differences and

act accordingly. In most cases colour and cloudiness are not a problem. But, in rare instances, it might mean referring the donor to their GP, or in the case of possible bacterial contamination, not using the donation, just to be on the safe side.

So, the next time you tuck into an oily curry the night before you donate, have a think about what colour your blood might be.

Did you know...

The importance of blood colour has endured through history, surviving in expressions we use today. The term 'blue-blooded', implying that someone is royal, was taken from the Spanish sangre azul and was adopted by the English in the 1830s. The English aristocracy spent little time outdoors in the sunlight and powdered and painted their skin white. Commoners believed that aristocrats had blue blood in their veins as this was how the veins appeared through such pale, translucent skin. Another well-known expression, 'red-blooded', now means 'vigorous' or 'virile' but may have originated from male warriors returning from battle and being bloodied.

Merlot and **claret** are both types of red wine.

This is an extract from a GCSE Science textbook. It explains about the chemical properties of blood.

A recipe for blood

On average a human adult has about five litres of blood inside them. About 40% of blood is made up of blood cells. There are three kinds of blood cell.

Red blood cells

There are 25 million million of these in an adult's body. They contain the red pigment haemoglobin and their main function is to carry oxygen from the lungs to the cells of the body. These cells live for about four months and are continually replaced.

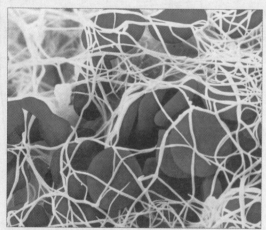

Red blood cells in a blood clot. The white material is strands of fibrin – the basis of the clot.

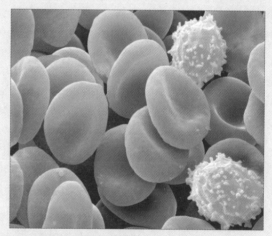

Two white blood cells in a sea of red blood cells. You can clearly see their different structure and shape.

White blood cells

These are the cells of defence and are fewer in number than red blood cells. There are two types: the phagocytes which eat disease organisms (microbes) and the lymphocytes which produce antibodies that act like chemical missiles against disease.

Platelets

These are tiny bodies in the blood that help to clot the blood. If the skin is damaged or cut this can let microbes in, so an emergency repair system quickly comes into action. Once a blood vessel is damaged the blood starts to leak out. When platelets come into contact with the air they break open. This causes a chain of reactions involving other chemicals in the blood (blood proteins) that leads to a clot forming in the damaged area.

Plasma

The other 60% of blood is a fluid called **plasma**. This is an almost colourless liquid (slightly yellow) that contains an enormous amount of substances such as:

- Water

- Dissolved food (glucose, amino acids, fats)

- Waste products (carbon dioxide, urea)

- Minerals

- Antibodies

- Blood clotting proteins

- Hormones

The bone marrow produces about 200 000 million red blood cells each day. Before a red blood cell dies it will have made about 172 000 journeys around the body. The blood vessels of the average adult would stretch almost $2\frac{1}{2}$ times around the Earth (about 95 000 km) if they were unravelled.

pigment = colouring

This is an extract from the first Sherlock Holmes novel, *A study in scarlet*, by Sir Arthur Conan Doyle. It was first published in 1887 and is narrated by Dr. Watson. This is the first time Dr. Watson has met Holmes, and they are introduced by Mr. Stamford.

This was a lofty chamber, lined and littered with countless bottles. Broad, low tables were scattered about, which bristled with retorts, test-tubes, and little Bunsen lamps, with their blue flickering flames. There was only one student in the room, who was bending over a distant table absorbed in his work. At the sound of our steps he glanced round and sprang to his feet with a cry of pleasure. "I've found it! I've found it," he shouted to my companion, running towards us with a test-tube in his hand. "I have found a re-agent which is precipitated by haemoglobin, and by nothing else." Had he discovered a gold mine, greater delight could not have shone upon his features.

"Dr. Watson, Mr. Sherlock Holmes," said Stamford, introducing us.

"How are you?" he said cordially, gripping my hand with a strength for which I should hardly have given him credit. "You have been in Afghanistan, I perceive."

"How on earth did you know that?" I asked in astonishment.

"Never mind," said he, chuckling to himself. "The question now is about haemoglobin. No doubt you see the significance of this discovery of mine?"

"It is interesting, chemically, no doubt," I answered, "but practically …"

"Why, man, it is the most practical medico-legal discovery for years. Don't you see that it gives us an infallible test for blood stains. Come over here now!" He seized me by the coat-sleeve in his eagerness, and drew me over to the table at which he had been working. "Let us have some fresh blood," he said, digging a long bodkin into his finger, and drawing off the resulting drop of blood in a chemical pipette. "Now, I add this small quantity of blood to a litre of water. You perceive that the resulting mixture has the appearance of pure water. The proportion of blood cannot be more than one in a million. I have no doubt, however, that we shall be able to obtain the characteristic reaction." As he spoke, he threw into the vessel a few white crystals, and then added some drops of a transparent fluid. In an instant the contents assumed a dull mahogany colour, and a brownish dust was precipitated to the bottom of the glass jar.

"Ha! ha!" he cried, clapping his hands, and looking as delighted as a child with a new toy. "What do you think of that?"

"It seems to be a very delicate test," I remarked.

"Beautiful! beautiful! The old Guiacum test was very clumsy and uncertain. So is the microscopic examination for blood corpuscles. The latter is valueless if the stains are a few hours old. Now, this appears to act as well whether the blood is old or new. Had this test been invented, there are hundreds of men now walking the earth who would long ago have paid the penalty of their crimes."

"Indeed!" I murmured.

"Criminal cases are continually hingeing upon that one point. A man is suspected of a crime months perhaps after it has been committed. His linen or clothes are examined, and brownish stains discovered upon them. Are they blood stains, or mud stains, or rust stains, or fruit stains, or what are they? That is a question which has puzzled many an expert, and why? Because there was no reliable test. Now we have the Sherlock Holmes' test, and there will no longer be any difficulty."

medico-legal = a combination of medical and legal evidence that can be used in law

infallible = something that cannot fail or be wrong

bodkin = a sharp instrument, a bit like a long pin

corpuscles = blood cells

1 In the section headed **Colour match**, why do staff at the National Blood Service centres look out for darker donations?

_____

_____

(1 mark)

2 Look again at the first paragraph, in the box. Explain why this has been placed at the beginning of the article.

_____

_____

_____

_____

_____

_____

_____

(2 marks)

3 Look again at the information in the box. Why are the staff described as 'scientific'?

_____

_____

(1 mark)

4 This article also explains what can be learned from the colour of plasma:

Plasma is usually a clear yellow. However, it can look cloudy occasionally. This can be caused by a number of things. You could simply have eaten some fatty food before giving blood, or it could be caused by an underlying condition related to high fat content in the body. It may even indicate a problem with the donation with regard to bacteria.

   a How does the writer show that you cannot draw a direct conclusion from the colour of plasma?

_____

_____

_____

(2 marks)

b Why has the writer done this?

_____

_____

(1 mark)

5 The article is taken from a booklet sent to people registered as blood donors.
Why was the article included in the booklet?
You should comment on:
- The subject matter of the article
- The way it has been written
- The presentation and layout

_____

_____

_____

_____

_____

_____

_____

_____

_____

_____

_____

_____

_____

_____

_____

_____

_____

_____

_____

_____

_____

(5 marks)

6 Why are platelets so important?

_____

(1 mark)

7 The information on these pages is intended to help GCSE students learn about Biology.
  a Explain why each paragraph is given a heading and how this helps the reader of the textbook.

_____

_____

(1 mark)

  b Explain why bullet points are used in the section headed **Plasma**, and how this helps the reader of the textbook.

_____

_____

(1 mark)

8 The writer has used brackets several times in this extract.
  a Identify and write down an example of brackets being used.

_____

(1 mark)

  b Explain why brackets are used in this way.

_____

_____

_____

(1 mark)

9 Why has this text been written? What is the writer trying to do?

_____

_____

_____

(1 mark)

10 How does the extract make this topic easy for the reader to follow?
You should comment on how the extract:
- Uses structural and layout devices
- Makes use of technical language and numbers
- Uses sentence structures.

_____

_____

_____

_____

_____

_____

_____

_____

_____

_____

_____

_____

_____

_____

_____

_____

_____

_____

_____

_____

_____

_____

_____

_____

_____

(5 marks)

Questions 11–14 are about *A study in scarlet*, by Sir Arthur Conan Doyle (pages 128–129).

11 What does Watson think of Holmes? Use a quotation to support your answer.

_____

_____

_____

_____
(2 marks)

12 Why does Holmes think his discovery is so important?

_____

_____

_____
(1 mark)

13 'This was a lofty chamber, lined and littered with countless bottles.'
What does the choice of language suggest about the room in which Holmes is working?

_____

_____

_____

_____
(2 marks)

14 What impression of Sherlock Holmes do you get from this extract?

_____

_____

_____

_____

_____

_____

_____

_____

_____

_____

_____

_____

(5 marks)

Writing skills

There's a lot more to being a great writer than just putting words in sentences and paragraphs!

Being a great writer means you are able to really think about what you are trying to say and how you are going to say it. There are lots of different sorts of writing and a great writer has to be able to be imaginative, interesting and thoughtful so their reader wants to read to the end, and sometimes even be left wanting more.

Great writers produce appropriate texts that are **organised** for greatest impact and can be followed by their readers. This includes features such as beautifully crafted sentences in logical and coherent paragraphs, and, of course, technical accuracy that includes spelling. Great writers also really think about their **vocabulary** and try to pick the best words – not necessarily the longest but the ones that do exactly what you want them to.

All of these features of a great writer have been broken down into different Assessment Focuses for KS3 and you will encounter them during your English lessons and in your Teacher Assessment at the end of Year 9.

Writing Assessment Focuses

AF1: write imaginative, interesting and thoughtful tasks
This means your work is interesting to read and shows your ideas.

AF2: produce texts which are appropriate to task, reader and purpose
This means your work is suitable for the intended audience, purpose and text type.

AF3: organise and present whole texts effectively, sequencing and structuring information, ideas and events
This means your ideas are easy to follow and develop in a logical way.

AF4: construct paragraphs and use cohesion within and between paragraphs
This means you use paragraphs and it is easy for the reader to see how each paragraph leads on to the next one. It is only assessed in the longer writing task.

AF5: vary sentences for clarity, purpose and effect
This means you construct your sentences to help convey your ideas. For example, you might use a very short simple sentence after a build-up of complex sentences to create contrast and impact.

AF6: write with technical accuracy of syntax and punctuation in phrases, clauses and sentences
Your word order is correct and your sentences say exactly what you want them to.

AF7: select appropriate and effective vocabulary
This means you choose carefully the best words for your writing.

AF8: use correct spelling
This is only assessed in the shorter writing task.

The tasks

This part of your KS3 English pack contains lots of different tasks for you to work through. Each task relates to the Assessment Focuses to ensure you practise all eight to be brilliant in your English lessons and your final Teacher Assessment.

It doesn't matter how long you spend on these tasks – in fact, it's better to take the time you need to make sure your answers are brilliant! To check your answers, turn to the back of the book.

When you get to the longer writing tasks you will need to work out the **purpose**, **audience** and **text type** before you start to plan. This will help you to work out exactly how to craft your response. It's really good to get into the habit of using this skill whenever you are reading or writing as it will help ensure you are great at both.

The writing questions all follow the same sort of format:

Arts for all

> The title of the task – this doesn't have to be the title you use.

You are employed by a local theatre to organise an arts festival every year.

You are about to plan this year's festival so decide to look at some feedback forms from last year's event.

> The role you need to adopt. This will affect the tone of your writing. It also gives you an idea about the purpose and audience.

Arts Festival
- There were lots of great activities for the 3–7 age range.
- You needed to provide more cleaning facilities, my kids got paint all over the car on the journey home.
- The festival is just for kids but adults need art too!
- The end of festival exhibition and production was fantastic. What a sense of achievement.

> Scene setting – ideas to get you thinking. You can add your own ideas to the ones you are given.

Write a report for your team to explain your plans for this year's festival.

(30 marks)

> Your actual task. It tells you purpose, audience and text type. In this case that's:
> **Purpose:** to explain
> **Audience:** your team at the theatre
> **Text type:** a report

Purpose, audience and text type

1 Read these text extracts and match each one to its intended audience and purpose (see opposite).

1 I wish to highlight the appalling state of the roads in my town. There are huge potholes which are not only uncomfortable but dangerous to all road users. Yesterday, I saw a cyclist fall off his bike after his front wheel went down one of these traps. Action is needed …

2 Good morning.

I would like to speak to you this morning about our need for proper cycle paths to school. We all know that cycling to school is fast and healthy, but only if we are not in danger from lorries and cars thundering past, threatening to knock us over.

Cycle paths could be our safe route to school, but we need to fight for them and that's where you come in …

3 Secondly, if the school were to provide safer cycle sheds more students would cycle to school, which would reduce the traffic around the school and make the roads safer for everyone. This is a benefit the school cannot ignore as it would also have a positive environmental impact …

4 Thank you for your interest in our Premium Cycle Sheds. I enclose a comprehensive brochure detailing the different models and options available and would like to draw your attention to the following points that make our product the market-leader:
- Value for money
- Designed to fit your school's needs
- Sturdy and secure
- Long-lasting and guaranteed for ten years

Our customers often find the best way to make a decision is with the help of one of our experts, and I am pleased to confirm that Lilly George will be happy to come and visit you to explain your options ...

5 Issues with the Premium Cycle Shed

Claims on the ten year guarantee are high, with specific problems related to rust and corrosion. The cost to upgrade the materials to prevent this problem is roughly equal to the cost of repairs following claims. However, the increased product confidence and potential sales implication would make this route valuable.

Proposal

Upgrade materials ….

Intended audience

a Your head teacher
b Potential customer
c Your whole year group
d Project manager
e Local council members

Purpose (you might find the texts have more than one purpose)

i Persuade, argue, advise
ii Inform, explain, describe
iii Imagine, explore, entertain
iv Analyse, review, comment

Text	Intended audience	Purpose
1		
2		
3		
4		
5		

2 There are problems with these cycle sheds. Imagine you are the head teacher and you are not happy with the Premium Cycle Sheds you purchased for your school last year.

On a separate sheet of paper, write your letter of complaint to the company.

3 Now try identifying the **purpose, audience** and **text type** in this task.

Local radio star

You work as a radio presenter for your local radio station. You are going to the monthly meeting to suggest new ideas to make the radio station more interesting for young people in your area.
Your research has found the following:

Local radio for local teens
• Include information about local events for teenagers
• Have local teenage voices presenting – we don't want an adult telling us what to think
• Don't be afraid to raise difficult issues
• A good mix of new music, perhaps from local bands
• A review of gadgets and new stuff

Write a report to advise the radio station controller what to include in the new programme for teenagers.

Purpose _____

Audience _____

Text type _____

Using the right words

1 Amazing adjectives

Look at these adjectives. They can all be used to describe your tests.
Sort them into the correct column in the table.

> stimulating boring tedious essential exciting challenging
> interesting mundane ordinary dull normal wearisome
> vital crucial monotonous necessary commonplace usual

negative	neutral	positive
dull		

2 Vary your verbs

How many other words can you think of to replace these verbs?

a go _____

b said _____

c sleep _____

d cry _____

e walk _____

3 Use Standard English

How would you change these if you were giving a formal presentation?

a This product is really *cool*. _____

b I'll *catch* you later. _____

c I *dunno* what to suggest. _____

d *Hi ya!* _____

e We don't want to be *ripped off*. _____

4 Add some pictures

Can you think of any similes you can use to describe the following?

a a really fierce deputy head teacher _____

b a jolly and cheerful footballer _____

c a huge grey factory _____

d a small boat out at sea _____

e a child skiing down a mountain _____

5 Tug at the heart-strings

Can you change these phrases to make them more emotive?

a Young man hits old woman.

_____

b The Guildford Flames beat their opposition.

_____

c When the sun is shining I enjoy a cold drink.

_____

d We have to stay inside the house because there is too much snow around.

_____

e The old cat tried to catch a bird and failed.

_____

6 Know when to avoid bias

Can you change these emotive phrases into neutral ones?

a The bear ripped him to shreds.

_____

b The woodland was ravished by a terrifying blaze.

_____

c He shovelled the greasy burger into his mouth as if he was starved.

_____

d She shrieked as the thug yanked the handbag from her arm.

_____

e The crumbling school buildings are a death-trap.

_____

Sentence structures

1 Add some complexity

Re-write these extracts, changing the sentence structure to make them more powerful and coherent.

a I am very excited. I am going on holiday to America tomorrow. My whole family are going. What's really good is that I am allowed to take my best friend.

_____

_____

_____

b Cats are natural predators. When they see a bird or mouse it just means excitement to them. Sometimes they kill without the desire to eat their prey. Some cats can be shocked when they catch something.

_____

_____

_____

_____

2 Watch the length

These sentences are out of control. Re-write them, putting in punctuation to make the meaning clearer.

a The market was full of exciting smells and colours and noises and people and new things.

_____

_____

b Music can create the atmosphere you need to learn and it can even help you to remember ideas because when you come to revise you can listen to the same music and it will help you to recall the original idea because your memory has made a link.

_____

_____

_____

_____

_____

_____

3 Zoom into the action

Look at this sentence:

> In the shadows, under the stairs, resting against the chair was a bloody knife.

The reader is taken closer and closer to the really important discovery of the knife by the phrases that start the sentence.

Complete these sentences to zoom your reader into the action!

a At the end of the garden, beyond the tree was _____ .

b In the car, sitting quietly as directed, _____ .

c In the corner of the room, _____

_____ .

d Under the floorboards, _____

_____ .

4 Add layers of meaning

A complex sentence has a main clause and one or more subordinate clauses:

> They ate chocolates greedily, until they felt sick.

The main clause, 'They ate chocolates greedily' can be understood by itself but the subordinate clause, 'until they felt sick' doesn't make sense by itself.

Underline the main clause in red and the subordinate clause in blue, in these sentences.

a I hid under the duvet shaking, as the storm raged outside.

b Claire, who was filled with a sense of relief, left the stage.

c Until the power cut hit, Paul refused to leave his computer.

Re-write these as complex sentences. You might choose to put the subordinate clause at the beginning, in the middle or at the end.

d Sally loved the book. She missed her bus because she was reading it. _____

_____

e The computer finally died. It had been used non-stop. _____

_____

f Amanda bought some new pink shoes. She loved shopping. _____

_____

Paragraphs and structure

1 Read this extract and mark where the paragraphs should go.
You might want to change the order.

When you first see my house you might think it's a bit dull and dingy because there are plants growing up the front wall and the path is a bit overgrown. I like to think this adds character and makes it more exciting when you come and visit me. If I trust you, and the others say it's OK, I might take you to the end of the garden to see our den. It's taken us years to create it and it's simply the best place to be in the summer. Once you are in you'll probably be drawn into the kitchen as there's generally something good cooking and that's where we tend to be. It's funny really, as it's the smallest room in the house but it's where we spend our time together. (Well, not the smallest, but you wouldn't all sit round the bathroom to talk about the day, would you?) Stepping through the front door for the first time is normally a bit of a shock because we've painted the inside really bright colours. The woodwork (that's the doors and skirting boards) is pink and the walls are purple. My gran hates it, but we sat down and made a family decision so it's fine by us.

2 You also need to start new paragraphs when there's a new speaker. Mark the paragraph breaks in this extract with a forward slash (/).

"Look, I'm really sorry," said Barry with frustration, "but this is just not going to work and that's an end to it." He threw down the play script and stood up to go. Laura looked up at him. "I'm really sorry as well," she said with sarcasm, "I'm really sorry that we've wasted so much time rehearsing with you in the lead role when we could have had Lance. He would at least have listened to our ideas." "That's just typical, " replied Barry, "and that's why I'm leaving. You've never wanted me in this stupid play. Well, if you think Lance will have anything to do with you when he hears how you've treated me you've got another think coming!" The rest of the cast sat watching with amazement as he coolly collected his jacket and walked out of the rehearsal room. Laura sat stunned. "Did that really just happen?" she asked, "Did we finally get rid of that idiot?" "Yes!" shouted Sian with joy. "Well done, you finally did it!"

3 Choose the appropriate connectives from the list and add them to the recipe below.

Next   Finally   Then   Secondly   Firstly

_____ pre-heat the oven to 180°.

_____ take your vegetables and chop them into 1 cm size cubes.

_____ lightly oil the baking tray and arrange the vegetables on it so they are evenly spaced.

_____ put the tray in the oven and set the timer to 40 minutes.

_____ remove the vegetables from the oven and enjoy!

Writing in different formats

1 Look at the text types in the box and the list of writing elements below. Match the most likely text type (or types) to each element.

> letter   newspaper   story   leaflet   report   speech

- Your address in the top right

  _____

- Impersonal phrases

  _____

- The date

  _____

- Snappy headline

  _____

- Alliteration

  _____

- Short paragraphs

  _____

- Bullet points

  _____

- Sign-off of 'Yours faithfully, Yours sincerely' or a more informal phrase if you know the person

  _____

- Rhetorical techniques

  _____

- Entertain and inform

  _____

- Informal style

  _____

- Repetition

  _____

- Clear but lively

  _____

- Factual

  _____

- Formal address

  _____

- Short sentences

  _____

- Clear statement of purpose

  _____

- Sub-heading

  _____

- Modal verbs

  _____

- Emotive language

  _____

- Personal pronouns

  _____

- The address of the person you are writing to in the top left

  _____

- Formal style

  _____

- Quotations from experts

  _____

- Pattern of three

  _____

- Varied length of sentences

  _____

2 Label these features in the newspaper article below.

> headline   sub-heading   use of expert   illustration   caption

PET FISH FRIED
Fish lover left red-faced

Paul Roberts, fish owning expert, was left red-faced yesterday, after he managed to fry hundreds of pounds worth of Koi Carp.

Roberts, who travels the world advising on the care of these creatures, fitted his own water filter system, something he advises his readers to leave to the professionals.

Unfortunately, he made a fatal error with the wiring and managed to heat his pond to near-tropical temperatures! The poor fish didn't stand a chance, as their home boiled and then exploded.

The stone pond exploded under the pressure of the boiling water and the boiled carp were sent flying. "My cat thought it was wonderful as cooked fish came flying through the air" explained Roberts' neighbour, Brian Downing, "although it was a horrendous noise!"

Roberts wasn't available for comment, but his wife said he was shocked and very saddened.

£400 Koi cat food

3 Now find these features in the speech below.

> emotive language   repetition   alliteration   list of three

" Everybody knows that litter is dirty and dangerous. So why do we just drop our litter?

Rats are attracted to places with lots of litter, such as our school. Now, you might have an idea of rats as cute and cuddly, but they actually spread dangerous diseases such as cholera, typhus and leptospirosis. We do not want these around our school, so why do we just drop our litter?

We need to make a stand. We need to make a difference. You need to make a difference.

Firstly, take responsibility for your own actions. Put your litter in a bin or your bag.

Secondly, take responsibility for our community. Challenge anyone you see dropping litter. Explain what the consequences could be and ask them to put their litter in a bin.

Finally, if you see a piece of litter, don't walk over it: deal with it. By doing this you will make a difference. "

Punctuation

1 Write these sentences correctly.

a i am going to the shop to buy some crisps my dog needs to walk

_____

_____

b the shopping centre banned teenagers as they were bad news they thought

_____

_____

c james and amanda are going to france to learn to ski i hope they enjoy it

_____

_____

d i can't believe top of the pops is still going after all these years it's really amazing

_____

_____

e my english teacher is going to be really impressed with my improved writing skills

_____

_____

2 Use commas, dashes, colons, semi-colons and brackets to improve these sentences.

a You will need a pen a pencil and a ruler.

_____

b I had a great birthday thanks.

_____

c Jane likes Shakespeare Caroline prefers modern drama.

_____

d The bread which was actually put out for the birds had been eaten by the cat.

_____

_____

3 Shorten these words using an apostrophe.

a I am _____

b it is _____

c they are _____

d you are _____

e we are _____

4 Remove the apostrophe from these words and write them out in full.

a he's _____

b let's _____

c could've _____

d can't _____

e we've _____

5 Re-write these sentences using an apostrophe to show ownership.

a The cats which belonged to Lucy were hungry.

_____

b Let's all go round to the flat belonging to Wayne for a party.

_____

c I won all the prizes at the sports day belonging to my school.

_____

d The provision for young people provided by my town is inadequate.

_____

e The car belonging to my brother is a heap of junk.

_____

Spelling

1 Plurals

Change these words into plurals.

a bus   buses

b try

c potato

d church

e child

f sheep

g fox

h car

i tomato

j business

k calf

l rush

2 Present to past

Write the present participle and past tense of these verbs.

a to run   running   ran

b to stop

c to drop

d to decide

e to watch

f to form

g to admit

h to prefer

i to benefit

j to state

k to fight

l to begin

3 Misspellings

Write these words correctly.

a acomodation _____ **i** peple _____

b asessment _____ **j** recieve _____

c audince _____ **k** secondery _____

d buisness _____ **l** seperate _____

e embarase _____ **m** sincerly _____

f explaination _____ **n** serprise _____

g intresting _____ **o** tommorow _____

h marrage _____ **p** wierd _____

4 Beware of homophones

Underline the correct word in these sentences.

a Lance and Susan are looking forward to **they're / there / their** holiday.

b "**Who's / Whose** homework is this?" asked the teacher. "It doesn't have a name!"

c The old house was very creepy at night because it was so **quiet / quite**.

d "You may all go to lunch **accept / except** Katie."

e You need to explain the **effect / affect** of the metaphor.

f Oh, look! My pen is over **they're / there / their**.

g "**Who's / Whose** up for swimming?" asked Andrea.

h I was **quiet / quite** pleased with my homework but the teacher didn't seem impressed.

i I've got to go up in assembly to **accept / except** a prize on behalf of my tutor group.

Writing to review: shorter writing task

Poor Luke!

You receive the following email from a friend who is recovering in hospital following an operation.

New Message

| Send | New | Attach | Find | Font | Print |

To:

Subject:

Hello there, thanks for your last email. I think I would die of boredom without your emails. I can't believe I'm only allowed to use the computer for half an hour a day! Oh well, got to share it, I suppose.

I'm having to spend time reading now, and I'm really getting into it. Have you read any good books or seen any good films lately? I'd love to hear about something you think I should read or watch.

Right, got to go now. I look forward to hearing from you!

All the best

Luke

> Don't forget you have to use Standard English, even though this is an email to a friend.

Write an email to Luke in which you review a book or film you think he will enjoy.

(20 marks including 4 marks for spelling)

> You are not provided with a planning sheet for the shorter writing task but you still need to plan!

Writing to comment: shorter writing task

Be the spokesperson!

Your school has conducted a survey to see if its students want to keep or change their school uniform.

Here are the results:

17% of students don't want any kind of uniform.

20% of students want to keep the current uniform.

63% of students want to keep a uniform, but not the current one.

– Of these, the majority want a more varied uniform.

– There is also much support for the idea that Years 10 and 11 have a slightly different uniform from Years 7–9.

The sixth form don't want a uniform at all.

The head teacher would like you to comment on these results so that the Leadership Team know what action to take.

Write your commentary on these results.

(20 marks including 4 marks for spelling)

You are not provided with a planning sheet for the shorter writing task but you still need to plan!

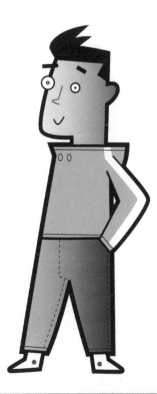

Writing to describe: shorter writing task

Celebrating past lives

Older people can be inspiring, interesting, scary or a mixture of all these things.

- What have they seen/experienced?
- How has this affected them today?
- What do you think about them?

Think about an old person you know or have heard about, and write a detailed description of them.

(20 marks including 4 marks for spelling)

You are not provided with a planning sheet for the shorter writing task but you still need to plan!

Writing to explain: shorter writing task

Holiday decisions

Your family is trying to decide where to go on holiday.
You have found the following holiday:

Family favourite

Join us at Glowing Sands for the family holiday of a lifetime. There's so much to do, for all the family:

• **Relaxation zone** – calm and tranquil, for those chill-out times
• **Music zone** – live music, karaoke and the club. Music and performance lessons are available; who knows, maybe you'll be on the stage at the end of the week?
• **Art zone** – think, look, create. Express the artist in you.
• **Beauty zone** – pamper your body and make sure it's a whole new you at the end of the week.
• **Nature zone** – for those who like to get out and about – the beauty of our natural setting awaits. From nature walks, to getting to grips with your gardening.
• **Sea zone** – develop your skills on the sea. Windsurfing, sailing and diving are all available.

Decide if you would like to go on this holiday or not.

Write your ideas down to explain them.

(20 marks including 4 marks for spelling)

You are not provided with a planning sheet for the shorter writing task but you still need to plan!

Writing fiction: Longer writing task

New worlds, new experiences

You are writing a story about the first landing on a new planet.

Your characters have been travelling in space for over a year and have finally landed on this new planet.

Below are some notes you have made for the next chapter of this novel.

Notes for chapter about landing on Planet X

Include:

- How the characters feel after travelling for over a year

- Worries and concerns they have about what is about to happen

- Their first reaction to Planet X

Character notes:

- Ann is a 'get up and go' sort of person. She has found the journey really difficult.

- Afsheen is impatient to explore Planet X.

- Mark is very aware of the possible dangers of a new planet.

Write the next chapter of the novel.

(30 marks)

You may wish to use this page to plan your work.

(This page will not be marked.)

Don't forget to identify purpose, audience, text type!

- Notes about the journey and how the astronauts feel

- The conversation they have and the decisions they make before getting out

- The new planet – what they can see, hear, smell, taste, touch

- What happens when they get out of the spacecraft

Use lined paper to write your answer. You can assess your work by checking the sample levelled answers at the back of this book.

Writing to describe: Longer writing task

Local descriptions of local places

Your English teacher gives you the following and suggests you take part:

Local writers wanted to describe local places
WE NEED YOU!

We're publishing a new guide to the UK, but this time the entries are to be by people who really know their places. Rather than sending travel writers to visit your town for half a day and then write about it, we want to get the truth.

Write an entry for our new guidebook and you could see your work in our new book!

You will need to cover the following areas, but we want your description to be as interesting as possible:

• The setting and atmosphere

• Local life – what's going on there?

• The best bits

• Things that need to be changed

• Your overall impression.

Write a description of the place where you live, to enter the competition.

(30 marks)

You may wish to use this page to plan your work.

(This page will not be marked.)

- What does it look like, what can you see? What is the atmosphere like?

- Local events – what is there to do?

- The good things about living here

- The bad things about living here

- What I think of the place where I live.

Use lined paper to write your answer. You can assess your work by checking the sample levelled answers at the back of this book.

Writing to inform: Longer writing task

The next stages of my life ...

You have received a letter from a relative you don't see very often. Here is part of it:

> I enjoyed reading about your school play and am sorry I wasn't able to come and see you. I am really pleased it went so well.
>
> I do enjoy reading about your school life. I know it must be boring for you to have to write about it, but school seems so different from when I was there (I don't want to admit how many years ago that was). What else is happening there?

Write a letter to this relative telling them about your school life.
Do not include an address.

You might like to use one or more of the following ideas:

• Your option choices for Year 10

• Your extra-curricular activities

• Your lessons

• How your school day is organised

(30 marks)

You may wish to use this page to plan your work.

(This page will not be marked.)

Don't forget to identify purpose, audience, text type!

• Ideas to open the letter and my response to the letter I was sent

Ideas to include in reply		
• The decisions I've had to make about my options	• The decisions I made and my reasons	• The events and changes I'm looking forward to

Use lined paper to write your answer. You can assess your work by checking the sample levelled answers at the back of this book.

Writing to review: Longer writing task

Music with you all day long ...

You work for a magazine that reviews electrical gadgets. You have been sent a new revolutionary music player to review. Here are the specifications:

MusicWrap

At last, a music player that doesn't need wires!

Key specifications:

- It looks like a wristwatch and tells the time, but it also plays music!

- You can download up to 10,000 tracks onto it.

- The music quality is second to none.

- It's wrapped round your wrist so you won't lose it!

- You don't need wires! Wireless technology means you just clip the headphones to your ears.

- Easy to use, fabulous to listen to!

Write the review for your magazine.

(30 marks)

You may wish to use this page to plan your work.

(This page will not be marked.)

Don't forget to identify purpose, audience, text type!

- What do you think of the idea?

- How does the wristwatch player work? Benefits? Problems?

- How do the wireless headphones work? Benefits? Problems?

- Would you recommend it?

Use lined paper to write your answer. You can assess your work by checking the sample levelled answers at the back of this book.

Writing to advise: Longer writing task

Supermarket threat

You read this article in your local paper:

Skate threat from supermarket

Local planning officers were considering a planning application from a large supermarket yesterday. Foods 'R'Us has applied to build a new store where the skatepark currently is.

Although the store will provide lots of jobs and be very useful for local people there is already some opposition to it.

Local shopkeepers are worried their small shops will go out of business and local kids want to know where they are supposed to go if their skatepark disappears.

Planning officers have raised these issues with Foods 'R'Us and are awaiting their reply. In the meantime, they have asked local people to let them know what they think. Write to …

Write a letter to the planning officer to advise them what to do.
Do not include an address.

(30 marks)

You may wish to use this page to plan your work.

(This page will not be marked.)

Don't forget to identify purpose, audience, text type!

Advantages of the new supermarket being built	Disadvantages of the new supermarket being built
• More convenient shopping	• Loss of the skatepark
• More jobs	• Loss of local businesses

Use lined paper to write your answer. You can assess your work by checking the sample levelled answers at the back of this book.

Practice writing paper

Have a go at answering this practice writing paper.

Make sure you are in a quiet place and can spend 1 hour 15 minutes without being disturbed.

You need to keep an eye on the time so that you spend 45 minutes on the longer writing task and 30 minutes on the shorter writing task.

- Spend 15 minutes reading and planning the longer writing task. You are given a planning sheet. Although you don't *have* to use it, it does make sense to do so.

- Spend 25 minutes writing your answer to the longer writing task. This leaves you 5 minutes to go through checking, correcting and improving your work.

- Spend 10 minutes reading and planning the shorter writing task. Although you are not given a planning sheet, you still need to make a plan.

- Remember to spend 5 minutes going through and checking, correcting and improving your answer to this task.

Writing paper

Longer writing task

This is worth 30 marks and you should spend 45 minutes on it.

Shorter writing task

This is worth 20 marks, including 4 marks for spelling. You should spend 30 minutes on it.

You will need separate paper to answer these tasks.

Section A

Longer writing task

Money matters

You have just received the following information from the school governors:

> The governors are delighted to announce that Liz Day, a past student, has made a gift of £10,000 to the school.
>
> The governors would like to know what you, the students, think this money should be spent on. Some suggestions are listed below, or you can make your own suggestion:
>
> • Use the money to buy new computer equipment.
>
> • Buy new books for the library.
>
> • Spend it on a school visit for the whole school.
>
> • Build a statue of Miss Day to express thanks.
>
> • Develop the school's sports facilities.
>
> • Buy new musical instruments.

Write a letter to the governors to persuade them to spend the money on the project of your choice.

(30 marks)

Longer writing task

Planning page

You can use this page to make notes for your letter.

(This page will not be marked.)

- What should the money be spent on?

- Why is this a good project?

- Why is this better than other ideas?

- How will it benefit the whole school?

Shorter writing task

Teen TV

You receive a memo from your boss:

I've just received this data from our research team. It looks like we need a new programme for teenagers – to fill the 4–4.30 slot.

Have a look at the data and let me have your ideas as quickly as possible, please.

Research into new teenage show:

We need something new for 4–4.30.

- This is prime time for the teen market – they are home and could be in front of the TV.

- There was a positive response to the following content:
  - Live music
  - Magazine style
  - Fast competitions, for viewers to win something substantial

- There was a negative response to the following content:
  - Silly games
  - Adult presenters behaving like children
  - Competitions for studio guests

Our competitors fill this slot with cartoons, programmes aimed at the younger market and talk shows for adults We want a programme for the 13–16 audience.

What do you think? Write an outline of a TV programme that might be suitable for this audience and time slot.

(20 marks including 4 marks for spelling)

Reading and writing checklist

Reading

I am able to:

- Understand texts and find information in them ☐
- Describe what happens in a text ☐
- Select information to support my ideas ☐
- Provide quotations to support my ideas ☐
- Deduce and infer ideas from texts ☐
- Interpret texts to explain what an author means or wants us to think ☐
- Identify structural features such as connectives used to direct the reader ☐
- Explain how a text has been organised to direct the reader ☐
- Comment on presentation ☐
- Explain how writers have used language ☐
- Identify and explain writers' word choices ☐
- Identify and explain how writers have used techniques such as:
  - repetition ☐
  - rhetorical questions ☐
  - alliteration ☐
  - metaphor ☐
  - simile ☐
- Identify features that show what a writer's purpose is ☐
- Comment on a writer's purpose and viewpoint ☐
- Comment on the overall effect of the text on the reader ☐

Writing

I am able to:

- Write clearly and accurately, so my writing is easy to follow ☐
- Develop my writing in a thoughtful way ☐
- Match my writing to the intended audience ☐
- Match my writing to the purpose ☐
- Organise my writing so it makes sense and develops logically ☐
- Sequence my ideas for maximum impact on my reader ☐
- Write in clear paragraphs ☐
- Write in paragraphs that develop logically and make sense ☐
- Link my paragraphs using connectives ☐
- Use simple, compound and complex sentences to create maximum impact on my reader ☐
- Vary my sentences for clarity and purpose ☐
- Punctuate my sentences accurately ☐
- Choose appropriate and effective vocabulary ☐
- Use my imagination to write interesting texts ☐
- Use correct spelling ☐

Shakespeare skills

Your English lessons aren't just about Reading and Writing – you will also cover Literature.

There are some amazing authors published in English, but perhaps the most famous is Shakespeare and everyone studies him in KS3 and KS4. It's a great idea to learn how to read and write about Shakespeare now as you'll have to do it for GCSE in KS4. More importantly, it's good to study Shakespeare because his plays and poems are really, really good!

Shakespeare wrote 37 plays and hundreds of poems. We've focused on the plays here because you have to study one during KS3. The skills you learn from studying a Shakespeare play will help you with your reading, writing and study of all Literature texts.

Literature can appear to be complicated when you start to study it, so it's a good idea to break it down into different areas of focus. We have used four different areas in this section:

• Character and motivation
This means you have to understand the behaviour of the main characters. You need to know and explain why the characters behave as they do.

• Ideas, themes and issues
This means that you have to understand the particular ideas (such as love or revenge) that your play explores.

• The language of the text
This means looking at what Shakespeare's characters say, how they say it and the effect this has on the audience.

• The text in performance
This means understanding and explaining how the scenes would have been performed, and how you might put them on if you were the director.

You'll find a combination of tasks that help you to unpick and understand different aspects of the play you are studying. If the example isn't from your play, don't worry because the tasks can be completed for any play.

You'll also find tasks focused on the language. Lots of people find this a bit daunting, but take your time and try to say it aloud – that really can help to work out the exact meaning. When you are analysing the language try to be as specific as possible and don't be afraid to write down any ideas the words create for you.

The longer tasks are all organised in the same way and have been written to allow you to answer them no matter which play you are studying:

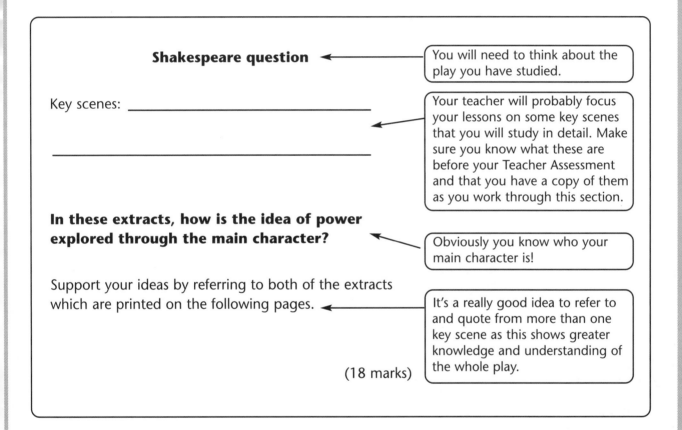

Shakespeare question ◄——— You will need to think about the play you have studied.

Key scenes: _____

_____

Your teacher will probably focus your lessons on some key scenes that you will study in detail. Make sure you know what these are before your Teacher Assessment and that you have a copy of them as you work through this section.

In these extracts, how is the idea of power explored through the main character?

Obviously you know who your main character is!

Support your ideas by referring to both of the extracts which are printed on the following pages. ◄———

It's a really good idea to refer to and quote from more than one key scene as this shows greater knowledge and understanding of the whole play.

(18 marks)

Preparing for the Shakespeare test

1 Fill in the information:

The play I am studying: —————————————————————

The key scenes I am studying: —————————————————————

The main characters in those scenes: —————————————————————

2 Character development

Look at the graph for your play. Track how each key character changes on this emotion graph. Use a different colour for each character to make it clear. You already have one character's changing emotions shown, to start you off.

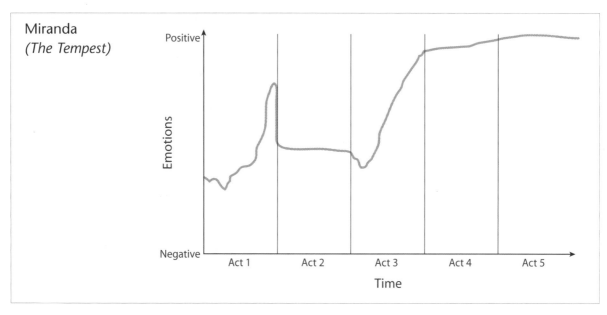

Miranda
(*The Tempest*)

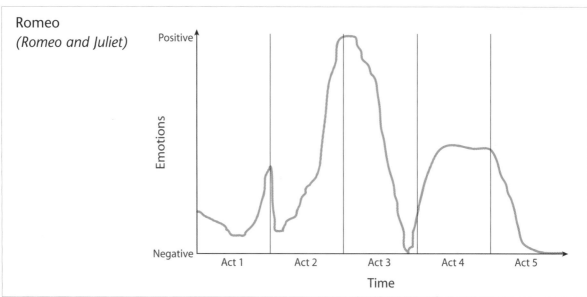

Romeo
(*Romeo and Juliet*)

3 Character analysis

Many characters in Shakespeare's plays are like icebergs – they don't show everyone what they are really like. Complete an 'iceberg' for each of your main characters.

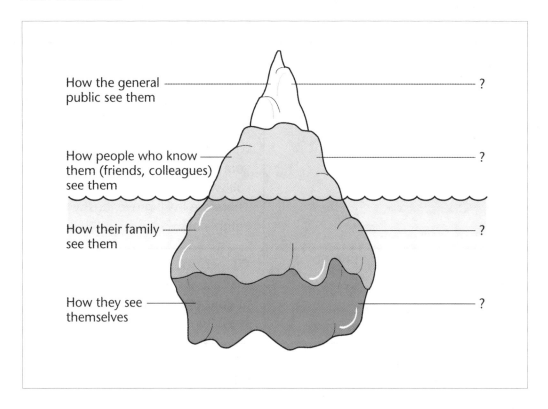

Try to find quotations to support your ideas at each level.

4 Understanding the scenes

You've focused on the characters; now think about the way Shakespeare has structured the scenes. Fill in this tension graph for each of your key scenes.

Shakespeare's language

The Tempest

1 Match the meanings

Draw lines to match the modern English versions with these quotations.

Shakespeare's words	Modern version
1 The fringèd curtains of thine eye advance, And say what thou see'st yond.	**A** I am chattering without control and forgetting my father's commands to ignore you.
2 Most sure the goddess On whom these airs attend!	**B** As soon as I saw you I fell in love with you and my heart became yours, to serve you. As my heart is still with you, I am slave to you. Therefore I will move logs without complaint.
3 But I prattle Something too wildly, and my father's precepts I therein do forget.	**C** Open your eyes, with their lashes that act as a fringe to the curtain of your eyelids, and say what you see before you.
4 The very instant that I saw you, did My heart fly to your service – there resides, To make me slave to it – and for your sake Am I this patient log-man.	**D** You must be the goddess that this music is played for

2 Analyse the language

Look at the quotations below. For each one, identify the language technique that has been used and explain the effect it has. The first one has been done for you.

> alliteration   metaphor   simile

Quotation	Technique	Effect
'the wild waves whist	alliteration of 'w'	Reflects the movement of the waves and spray.
'the fringèd curtains of thine eye'		
'thou shalt be as free / As mountain winds'		
'Poor worm, thou art infected!'		
'But you – o you, So perfect and so peerless – are created Of every creature's best'		

Romeo and Juliet

1 Match the meanings

Draw lines to match the modern English versions with these quotations.

Shakespeare's words	Modern version
1 Who set this ancient quarrel new abroach? Speak, nephew. Where you by when it began?	**A** Why does a name matter? What does a name mean? The flower we call a rose would still smell sweet if it had a different name.
2 So early walking did I see your son. Towards him I made, be he was ware of me, And stole into the covert of the wood.	**B** Don't swear by the moon because it changes every month. If you do, your love might also change all the time.
3 What's in a name? That which we call a rose By any other name would smell as sweet.	**C** Who started this old argument up again? Nephew, did you see it start? Tell me what happened.
4 O swear not by the moon, th' inconstant moon, That monthly changes in her circled orb, Lest that thy love prove likewise variable.	**D** I saw your son when I was out walking really early one morning. I went towards him, but he was aware of me and went into the wood where he was hidden from sight.

2 Analyse the language

Look at the quotations below. For each one, identify the language technique that has been used and explain the effect it has. The first one has been done for you.

> alliteration   oxymoron   metaphor   assonance

Quotation	Technique	Effect
'the bud bit with an envious worm'	alliteration of 'b'	Reflects the harsh and secret way the worm has infected the bud.
'O brawling love, O loving hate'		
'What light through yonder window breaks? It is the east, and Juliet is the sun'		
'love's light wings'		
'Love goes toward love as schoolboys from their books'		

Character and motivation

Choose the question that relates to the play you are studying. Use the space under the question to make notes and to write your plan. Write your actual answer on lined paper.

For more practice, you could have a go at answering the question(s) on the other play. Just substitute the name of the character.

Top Tip!

You need to make sure you cover both the scenes you are directed to. It's a good idea to mention events and ideas from outside these scenes, but you must make sure your focus is on the scenes you are given.

The Tempest

Focus on the key scenes of your play.

What impression do you get of Miranda in these scenes?

Support your ideas by referring to **at least two** of the scenes you have studied in detail.

(18 marks)

The Tempest

Focus on the key scenes of your play.

What impression do you get of Ferdinand in these scenes?

Support your ideas by referring to **at least two** of the scenes you have studied
in detail.

(18 marks)

Romeo and Juliet

Focus on the key scenes of your play.

How does Romeo change in these scenes?

Support your ideas by referring to **at least two** of the scenes you have studied
in detail.

(18 marks)

Themes

Choose the question that relates to the play you are studying. Use the space under the question to make notes and to write your plan. Write your actual answer on lined paper.

For more practice, you could have a go at answering the question(s) on the other play. Just substitute the theme.

The Tempest

Focus on the key scenes of your play.

How is the theme of love explored in these scenes?

Support your ideas by referring to **at least two** of the scenes you have studied in detail.

(18 marks)

Romeo and Juliet

Focus on the key scenes of your play.

How is the theme of love explored in these scenes?

Support your ideas by referring to **at least two** of the scenes you have studied in detail.

(18 marks)

Romeo and Juliet

Focus on the key scenes of your play.

How is the idea of deception explored in these scenes?

Support your ideas by referring to **at least two** of the scenes you have studied in detail.

(18 marks)

Language

Choose the question that relates to the play you are studying. Use the space under the question to make notes and to write your plan. Write your actual answer on lined paper.

For more practice, you could have a go at answering the question(s) on the other play. Just substitute the name of the character.

The Tempest

Focus on the key scenes of your play.

The language used in these scenes emphasises the high emotions experienced by the characters. Explain how Shakespeare has used the language to create this emotion.

Support your ideas by referring to **at least two** of the scenes you have studied in detail.

(18 marks)

Romeo and Juliet

Focus on the key scenes of your play.

Romeo and Juliet both play with language. Explain how Shakespeare uses language to show they are a good match.

Support your ideas by referring to **at least two** of the scenes you have studied in detail.

(18 marks)

Romeo and Juliet

Focus on the key scenes of your play.

Romeo's language is used to create his personality. Explain how Shakespeare does this.

Support your ideas by referring to **at least two** of the scenes you have studied in detail.

(18 marks)

The text in performance

Choose the question that relates to the play you are studying. Use the space under the question to make notes and to write your plan. Write your actual answer on lined paper.

For more practice, you could have a go at answering the question(s) on the other play. Just substitute the name of the character.

DiRector

Top Tip!

Don't forget, this is **not** about saying you want an actor to 'move to the front of the stage and look upset' – it is focused on **language**, not movement.

The Tempest

Focus on the key scenes of your play.

Ferdinand's emotions change dramatically in this play. Imagine you are directing this play. Explain how you want the actor playing Ferdinand to show his thoughts and emotions in these scenes.

Support your ideas by referring to **at least two** of the scenes you have studied in detail.

(18 marks)

The Tempest

Focus on the key scenes of your play.

The relationship between Prospero and Miranda is very important. Imagine you are directing this play and explain how you want the actors playing these characters to show their thoughts and emotions in these scenes.

Support your ideas by referring to **at least two** of the scenes you have studied in detail.

(18 marks)

Romeo and Juliet

Focus on the key scenes of your play.

Romeo's emotions change dramatically in this play. Imagine you are directing this play and explain how you want the actor playing Romeo to show his thoughts and emotions in these scenes.

Support your ideas by referring to **at least two** of the scenes you have studied in detail.

(18 marks)

Practice Shakespeare paper

Try this practice Shakespeare paper.

Make sure you are in a quiet place and can spend 45 minutes without being disturbed.

You need to keep an eye on the time so that you spend 10 minutes planning, 30 minutes writing your answer and 5 minutes checking and improving.

• You will need your copy of the key scenes.

• You will also need a pen and lined paper.

Shakespeare paper

This is worth 18 marks and you should spend 45 minutes on it.

This paper contains one task and you should answer it with reference to the key scenes of the Shakespeare play you have studied.

Answer the task that relates to the play you have studied.

The Tempest

Focus on the key scenes of your play.

Miranda's emotions change dramatically in this play. Imagine you are directing this play and explain how you want the actor playing Miranda to show her thoughts and emotions in these scenes.

Support your ideas by referring to **at least two** of the scenes you have studied in detail.

(18 marks)

Romeo and Juliet

Focus on the key scenes of your play.

What impression do you get of Romeo in these scenes?

Support your ideas by referring to **at least two** of the scenes you have studied in detail.

(18 marks)

You may use this page to plan your answer.

Shakespeare checklist

I am able to:

- Understand the events in the play ☐

- Understand the characters and their motivations ☐

- Describe what happens in my set scenes ☐

- Select key quotations to support my ideas ☐

- Make specific references to events in the play ☐

- Deduce and infer ideas from the events in the play ☐

- Identify structural features that add to the meaning of the play ☐

- Comment on stagecraft ☐

- Explain and comment on Shakespeare's use of language, including: ☐

    - metaphor ☐

    - simile ☐

    - alliteration ☐

    - onomatopoeia ☐

    - imagery ☐

    - repetition ☐

    - symbol ☐

- Explain the impact the text has on the audience ☐

Notes

Notes

Reading answers

pages 100–101

Purpose = to describe the setting and introduce the character
Audience = teenage readers of the book
Text type = prose, descriptive fiction writing

1 *Any one of:*

- 'Matt heard it and looked up briefly.'
- 'the crowd meant nothing to him.'
- 'He wasn't part of it.'
(1 mark)

2 The writer emphasises Matt's isolation by starting and ending the extract with a description of him by himself. The first sentence is actually a paragraph of its own, which makes it more of a striking statement. The final descriptions of him at the end of the extract are firstly a short statement and then a broken sentence. This sandwiching effect is contrasted with the chaos and confusion that is going on around him. The busy street is juxtaposed with Matt as an individual and helps to make him seem different and apart from it.
(2 marks, one each for any two of the above points)

3

Example of descriptive language	The impression it gives
'commuters were fighting their way out of the station.'	This gives the impression of pressure and chaos.
' a tangle of cars, taxis and pedestrians'.	Everything seems confused and busy.
' Somebody leant on their horn and the noise blared out'	The noise seems loud and ugly.

(1 mark for each up to a maximum of 2 marks)

4 Matt is made to seem isolated by the way he is set apart from the rest of the world and the language that has been used. The structure of the piece emphasises his isolation – he is described at the beginning and end of the extract and this description is juxtaposed with the busy commuter scene. Secondly, we are told he doesn't really react to what is going on around him, even though it is noisy and chaotic: 'Matt heard it and looked up briefly'. This suggests he is in a world of his own. Finally, we are told that the world around him is 'fighting' and a 'tangle' but he is just 'sitting'. This lack of movement makes him seem different and therefore isolated.
(3 marks. Notice there are three main points made. You would get a mark per point you make.)

5 It is clear that something bad is going to happen because we are told Matt knows he is 'making a mistake'. Perhaps he is going to do something that goes against the law or society. He is shown as being isolated, which suggests he does not feel like he is part of society, so maybe he doesn't care about doing something bad.
(2 marks)

pages 102–103

Purpose = to describe and entertain
Audience = teenage/adult readers of the book
Text type = prose, descriptive fiction writing

1 He is being told what to do by someone who has no right to do so.
(1 mark)

2 *Any two of:*
- 'narrowed his eyes'
- 'wished he were taller, stronger and eight years older'
- 'a ball of anger exploded inside him'
- 'made him wish he had the courage to say exactly what he wanted to say'
(1 mark)

3

Quotation	What it tells us about Bruno's state of mind
'Bruno narrowed his eyes and wished he were taller, stronger and eight years older'	Bruno is in a confrontational mood and wants to be as big, strong and old as the person he is angry with so that he can taken them on.
'A ball of anger exploded inside him'	This suggests a powerful knot of anger has been building up but it has now been let loose.

(1 mark each)

4 He doesn't like the Lieutenant telling him what to do and thinks he has no right to. He has very little respect for the Lieutenant, as shown by the sneering way he refers to his title as a 'fancy title'.
(1 mark)

5 Bruno is made to seem young by his use of the proper nouns 'Mother' and 'Father'. The fact he has not abbreviated them shows he is doing exactly as he is told and does not think of his parents in any way other than their relationship to him.
(2 marks)

6 The writer makes us take Bruno's side by focusing on his thoughts and feelings. We never learn what the Lieutenant thinks and that means we can't be as sympathetic towards him.

The description of the 'ball of anger' exploding shows us this exchange is really affecting Bruno. It suggests he has been trying to stop feeling angry for a long time but he has finally been pushed too far. However, he realises his limitations and his lack of courage: 'made him wish that he had the courage'. This also makes us side with him as it shows he is realistic and feels like he has no hope of standing up for himself.

The reference to 'Mother and Father', names which have been made into proper nouns to show these are the names by which Bruno thinks of them and refers to them, reminds us that Bruno is a young child. The fact he hasn't abbreviated these names suggests he is obedient and respectful towards his parents; characteristics which also make us take his side.

The language is very precise and careful, and we get the impression we are in Bruno's mind. When you follow a character's thought process you are more likely to side with them.
(5 marks)

pages 104–105

Purpose = to promote summer events in Woking
Audience = 7–16 year olds and their parents
Text type = magazine article

1

Activity	Details
drama workshop	Develop theatre skills, explore exciting scripts, meet others, final performance to friends and family
cinema crafts workshop	Make costumes and props, afternoon film
arts workshop	African drumming, Mexican crafts,
Craft Co. workshop	T-shirt painting, salt-dough modelling, card-making, pot-decorating
dance and poetry	Work with professional dancers, contribute your ideas, final performance

(2 marks, 1 from each column

2

Examples of language used	What it suggests
'a packed programme'	The alliteration makes it sound fun and exciting.
'a huge range of activities'	The adjective 'huge' emphasises the large amount of activities to choose from.
'chance to shine'	The verb 'shine' is positive and makes it sound like a brilliant opportunity.

(2 marks)

3 The article makes the opportunities seem exciting and attractive through the use of positive language, making it clear you can try new things, and by using bright colour and clear layout.

The activities are made to seem exciting and fun by language such as 'packed programme of activities' and 'get your creative juices really flowing'. The alliteration of the 'p' in 'packed programme' makes the phrase really bouncy and energetic, a bit like the activities they are trying to promote. The lists of activities also make it sound like there's lots to do which is really good when you're a teenager as you can get bored easily.

It might seem scary to join in with a workshop if you don't know anyone, but they mention the fact you can make new friends – 'meeting other young people'. This makes it seem more attractive as it's always good to meet other people with the same interests as you.

The presentation is attractive. The picture is of young people acting, which helps to show the

sort of things you might do. Bold print is used for each activity and this helps the reader as they can scan through the article and not have to read the bits they are not interested in.
(5 marks)

pages 106–107

Purpose = to persuade the reader to join LeisureTime Plus
Audience = Ms Holroyd/adults concerned about health and fitness
Text type = letter

1 Join LeisureTime Plus
(1 mark)

2 Ms Holroyd seems like someone who is interested in keeping fit and healthy but has not found it easy. Perhaps she has had a bad experience of gyms and fitness instruction.
(2 marks)

3 *Any two of:*
   • The letter uses statistics to support its claims about the value of exercise.
   • It provides a list of benefits, suggesting there are lots of good results to be had from exercise.
   • It uses positive language to describe the benefits of exercise.
   • It uses 'experts' to support its claims.
   (2 marks. Note, the question does not ask what the letter says, it asks about the methods used.)

4

Example of negative phrase	Why the language is used in this way
'crowded, sweaty gyms'	The negative adjectives make the gym sound horrible.
'sergeant-major fitness instructors with the bark of a bulldog'	The adjective 'sergeant-major' makes the fitness instructors sound strict and nasty. The 'bark of a bulldog' emphasises this impression.

(1 mark each)

5 *For example:*
   • Informal, colloquial phrase: 'a walk in the park'
   • Why it is used: it makes it sound like the writer of the letter is friendly and approachable. This colloquialism makes the whole letter seem informal and as if the writer knows how the reader will find exercise.
   (2 marks)

6 This letter makes joining LeisureTime Plus seem a good idea by making exercise seem like a vital part of life and explaining the benefits it might have. It uses opinion disguised as fact, 'Everybody knows the need to live a healthy lifestyle', to make its ideas seem logical and believable.

The letter has a friendly, approachable tone: 'but we'll be with you all the way'. This makes the company seem friendly and approachable which means the reader is more likely to join it.

It uses emotive language and the benefits of exercise are shown: 'fitter, healthier and happier'. This list of three makes it sound balanced. It also seems balanced and considered because it admits that exercise used to be unpleasant: 'crowded, sweaty gyms and sergeant-major fitness instructors with the bark of a bulldog'. Juxtaposing this with what LeisureTime Plus offers makes its product seem even better. It also seems more truthful because it admits how bad exercise used to be.

Finally, by addressing the reader directly, 'you'll notice', it makes it more personal which is effective.
(5 marks)

pages 108–109

Purpose = to inform of the decision to give mobile phones to schoolkids
Audience = adults
Text type = newspaper

1 *Any two of:*
   • Personal organisers
   • Record lessons
   • Set alarm to remind to do homework
   • Use the memo
   • Research using the Internet
   • Share ideas in class
   • Manipulate sounds in music
   • Morning alarm
   (1 mark for the two answers. $^1/2$ marks are not given.)

2 By the use of the connective 'However'. This tells us the information that follows will be different to the ideas that have already been presented.
(1 mark)

3 It suggests the world is modern and changing. The abbreviation 'techno' creates the impression of something fast-moving.
(1 mark)

4 Having a quotation from a named education advisor gives the story credibility and makes it seem more factual, despite the fact that he is just expressing an opinion.
(1 mark)

5 *Any two of the following. A total of two marks are available, one for each word or phrase selected with explanation.*
- 'claiming' suggests the teachers' view is just opinion and not correct
- 'constantly interrupting' makes the phones sound like a real ongoing nuisance
- 'demand' makes the teachers sound unreasonable
- 'dilapidated' emphasises the poor condition of the school buildings in an emotive way

(2 marks)

6 The views are not presented in a balanced manner. Firstly, the positive, government view is given more space and a quotation is included. Secondly, the teachers' views are presented with negative vocabulary and finally, the students aren't given a voice at all.

The mobile phone deal is presented in a positive way, with 'celebrating' by ministers and being described as 'a huge step forward'. These words and phrases create a positive impression of the deal and don't question it at all. Describing the world as 'techno' reminds the reader it is changing quickly and so learning must also change to keep up.

Wayne Daniels is presented as an expert and his views are presented as fact, giving the whole scheme credibility. The example of how students might use the phones to help organise themselves and make them do homework is a very positive view. Any potential negative outcomes are ignored totally. The phrase 'reel off lists of benefits' creates the impression that the benefits are so numerous that it's easy to list them.

The view of the teachers is presented very negatively after this innovation has been presented in such a positive way. We are told the teachers are 'claiming' and 'demand', words which sound very negative and aggressive. This tone makes us regard the teachers' view with suspicion.

Although the students are said to be 'celebrating', no student's view is reported so they aren't really given a voice. The use of the exclamation mark suggests that it's inevitable that students will celebrate and implies that the reporter didn't even go and interview them.
(5 marks)

pages 110–111

Purpose = to describe
Audience = teenage to adult
Text type = poem

1 The blackberries go mouldy and start to decay.
(1 mark)

2 It suggests they are desperate to collect all the blackberries so use any container they can get hold of.
(1 mark)

3 The final line, 'Each year I hoped they'd keep, knew they would not.' is balanced and shows that, although the narrator hopes they will keep, he knows they will rot. It gives the idea of a child clinging to hope when he or she knows deep down that time is passing and the natural world decays.
(1 mark)

4

Simile	Explanation
• 'hard as a knot'	This image describes how the unripe berries look and reminds us how hard and tightly formed they are. It also suggests they are dry and without their juice, as they are not yet ripe.
• 'like thickened wine'	This image makes the berry seem luscious and reminds us of its thick, potent juice.
• 'like a plate of eyes'	This is a horrible image and makes us think of the texture of the berries and the fact they have been stripped from the bush. They are shiny and reflecting all that is around them.
• 'palms sticky as Bluebeard's'	Bluebeard was a murderer, so this suggests the blackberry pickers are also murderers – they have picked all the berries, even though they know they won't keep.

(3 marks, one for a simile and two for its explanation)

5 The blackberry pickers seem eager, focused and hard-working. The speaker in the poem has a 'lust for picking', which suggests a desire you associate with a child rather then an adult. When the berries are ripe they use anything they can to collect them in, 'milk-cans, pea-tins, jam-pots', suggesting this is not an organised or professional harvesting. They don't mind the briars that scratch them as they are just focused on picking the berries.

The comment at the end, 'I always felt like crying' suggests the speaker was a child at the time of the blackberry picking, who hadn't yet learnt that the berries would rot and go off.
(5 marks)

6 The poet presents this memory as one that is good, but there is sadness mixed in with it. The excitement of the first 'glossy purple' blackberry creates 'lust', perhaps reflecting childish wonder at the natural world. However, there are many sinister images used in the poem which warn us that these wonderful berries are not the juicy treats they seem at first. We are told they are full of 'summer's blood' and there are other aspects of the natural world mentioned, such as the briars attacking them when they are picking the blackberries. This suggests they are robbing nature and shouldn't be taking so many berries.

By the end of the first stanza they have hands like 'Bluebeard's', likening them to a murderer. The sinister tone continues as we find the hoarded berries start to rot, 'rat-grey fungus, glutting on our cache'. Nature has won after all and although they have picked the berries they are not able to enjoy them all. Perhaps this is why there is a tone a sadness at the end of the poem. The adult poet looks back and realises it is not worth fighting nature. He is sad at his younger, naïve self, who will soon learn to stop hoping.
(5 marks)

pages 112–113

Purpose = to instruct the reader how to make a pizza
Audience = children/young people
Text type = recipe

1

Put the mozzarella on the pizza	2
Put your favourite toppings on the pizza	3
Make the tomato topping	1
Put the pizza in the oven	4

(1 mark)

2 This recipe is written for children or young cooks. I know this because of the language used such as 'fave' and 'scrummiest' and the way it suggests the reader gets an adult to help use the oven.
(3 marks)

3 *Any one of:*
  • First   • Now
  • Next   • When

These words are all connectives. They create a sense of order and logical progression. The reader knows not to move on to a new step before completing the previous one.
(3 marks)

4 *For example:*
  • 'How to make the scrummiest pizza'
  • 'our fave toppings'
  • 'plaster it with the tomato topping'
You'll also need an explanation along the lines of this one:
Using the abbreviation 'fave' makes this recipe seem fun and the author seem friendly. It's aimed at young cooks and it makes the writer seem like someone who will enjoy the same sort of food. Pizza is also a fun food so this word fits it well.
(2 marks)

5 It says 'Sometimes simple is best' because cheese and tomato sounds really boring when you think of all the toppings you could have on a pizza. It acknowledges this fact but reminds the reader that this classic topping is actually really nice.
(2 marks)

6 I think this text will make young people want to make the pizza. It makes the recipe seem fun by its use of colour and bright layout. It also uses language to make cooking seem exciting, for example 'fave' and 'mouth-watering'. It makes it clear that you can make the pizza with any toppings you like, 'there are no rules', and this sounds really creative and fun.

The text makes a connection with the reader by addressing them directly with the pronoun 'you' and by using language that the young cook might use with their friends, 'scrummiest' and 'fave'. This makes the reader think that the pizza is going to be suitable for a young person to eat and won't be boring food like you normally get in recipe books.

It also makes the recipe seem easy by using words such as 'plaster', which suggests you don't have to be really careful with everything, and saying 'there are no rules', which is really appealing for a young cook!
(5 marks)

pages 114–117

Purpose = to entertain
Audience = adults
Text type = prose fiction

1 He was in prison because he murdered his brother-in-law but he has now escaped.
(1 mark)

2 The jailer is called Burton Duff.   *(1 mark)*

3

Example of descriptive phrase	Impression it creates
'the moon sailed into a patch of unclouded sky'	The moon is free and moves easily. This contrasts with the actions of the fugitive.
'as white as death'	This simile suggests danger and evil and warns us that the figure pointing Orrin towards the jail might be a ghost.
'the livid mark of the iron bar'	The word 'livid' stands out just as the mark left by the iron bar. It is shocking and creates the impression of violence and danger.

(2 marks)

4a) The first sentence tells us that Orrin Brower comes from Kentucky, murdered his brother-in-law and has escaped from the law.
(1 mark)

b) It tells us lots of information very quickly to get us interested in the character and the story. It also means we know the background so the story can get going.
(1 mark)

5 *For example:*
'he saw, indistinctly, the figure of a man' or 'as white as death'.

You need an explanation such as:
The fact Orrin doesn't see his captor properly suggests something is strange about it. It doesn't speak to him, just points, and this is also unusual for someone capturing a wanted murderer.
(2 marks)

6 The author makes the ending of the story very dramatic through sentence lengths and repetition.

The penultimate paragraph is very detailed and this helps you to get a good picture of what is happening. The repetition of 'Straight' emphasises the fact that Orrin is not resisting arrest at all and is returning straight to jail. We are given lots of detail about him opening the door, 'laid his hand upon the knob of the heavy iron door', which slows the pace down and raises the tension and suspense. This is followed by two very short sentences, almost as if we are seeing the scene in real life and following Orrin's thought processes.

The final twist in the tale, that the person who captured Orrin and returned him to jail was the person he killed earlier in the story, is made even more shocking by putting it in a paragraph by itself. This makes it stand out more and so we spend more time reading it as it tells us Orrin was captured by a ghost.
(5 marks)

pages 118–119

Purpose = to review and entertain
Audience = anyone interested in film
Text type = review

1 *Be careful with this type of question! It wants to know more than that the film got 5 out of 5.*
The five stars show the reviewer likes the film and they make the reader want to know more about it. They are a quick and easy way for someone to find a review of a good film.
(1 mark)

2 *For example:*
- 'the poor long-suffering Gromit' which reminds us that Gromit is easy-going and bad things always happen to him.
- 'cheese-loving Wallace' which tells us more about Wallace and reminds us of his character traits.
(1 mark)

3 The repetition of 'big' builds up our anticipation and makes the film seem even better.
(2 marks)

4 *For example:*
Fact: it has been ten years since the last Wallace and Gromit film. *(Note you have to leave out the words 'long' and 'poor long-suffering' as these are opinions.)*

The reviewer starts the review with a fact embedded in opinion to make the whole review seem more factual. This will make us more likely to believe it.
(2 marks)

5 *For example:*
The phrase 'Maybe that means they weren't really needed?' is friendly and informal because it is as if the reviewer is just thinking aloud. This makes the reader think they are being very genuine and sincere, and we are reading their real thoughts.
(2 marks)

6 The positive language and tone of this review help to create the impression that this film is worth watching. Words such as 'Another' in the first line remind us that previous films have been fun to watch and suggest that if you enjoyed them you'd enjoy this one.

The use of exclamation marks creates a sense of excitement and this adds to the idea that the film is really good. Furthermore, words and phrases such as 'guaranteed to delight' are big claims and make it clear the reviewer likes the film, even without the five stars.

The reviewer includes positive language such as 'joy' and 'energy' to make this a positive review. Mentioning Computer Generated Imagery provides us with contrast and something to measure this film against. Recent CGI films have been really impressive, and this comparison is suggesting this film is even better.

The final sentence is a paragraph on its own which makes it stand out more. Finishing with the reminder that it won an Oscar helps to promote the film in a positive way.
(5 marks)

pages 120–121

Purpose = to promote the school and invite prospective parents to an open day
Audience = prospective parents
Text type = formal letter

1 The head has written this letter to promote the school and to invite prospective parents to an open day.
(1 mark)

2 The head mentions Oxbridge twice. This suggests he regards students getting into those universities as his greatest successes. He doesn't mention other school-leavers. It also suggests this is what he thinks the parents are interested in.
(2 marks)

3 The head uses 'we' to show that he represents the whole school. It makes it seem as if he can speak for the whole school and that they are a united community. He wants to create the impression that the school is working well as a community and that they all get on and want the same things.
(2 marks)

4 This letter uses short paragraphs to help categorise the information and make it easier for the reader to understand. It also makes it more formal as it makes it seem as if it is all very organised and there is no room for change.
(1 mark)

6 Bordondown School is made to seem very organised and successful with the mention of 'examination results' and Oxbridge. By saying they are looking forward to '<u>Another</u> year' of top results it implies previous years have been really successful.

The school also seems very strict. It mentions learning three times but gives examples about uniform and homework showing that it thinks

these are important. The phrase 'we find an organised student is a successful student' is almost robotic and reminds me of the Demon Headmaster! The use of the word 'insist' shows there is no choice.

It mentions 'many' extra-curricular activities, but it doesn't list any, instead it suggests the parent 'browse' through the prospectus. The word 'browse' is one of the only informal words here, perhaps suggesting that the head doesn't really know what activities are available?

Overall, the impression the letter creates of the school is one of an organised and strict place with good exam results.
(5 marks)

pages 122–135

1 Staff look out for darker donations because these might have bacterial contamination or have been stored incorrectly.
(1 mark)

2 *Any two of:*
  • Donors will read it before they read the article and it will reassure them the process is safe.
  • Donors will read it before they read the article and it will interest them in the whole article.
  • It reassures potential donors that the process is safe.
  • It outlines another safety check that is undertaken.
  • It makes the staff seem like trained experts.
  • It includes lots of safety checks.
  (2 marks)

3 Describing the staff as 'scientific' increases our trust in them and makes them seem like professional experts who know what they are doing.
(1 mark)

4a The writer uses modal verbs such as 'can', 'could' and 'may' to show you cannot draw a direct conclusion from the colour of plasma.
(2 marks – 1 for the term 'modal verb' and one for the use of examples. You do not need all three examples.)

4b *You might have one of the following ideas:*
  • The writer has done this to introduce ambiguity and show there are many possibilities.
  • It will ensure the reader does not jump to conclusions – it is too complex to do so.
  • It makes the whole process seem very complicated and the people who deal with it seem very skilled.
  (1 mark)

5 The subject matter is obviously going to be of interest to the audience as they are all blood donors. It has probably been included in this booklet to help explain what happens to the blood that is donated and to encourage people to keep being donors. It shows that the blood is really cared for and this implies how much it is needed.

The piece has been written in an informal but informative way. The facts give it authority and the rhetorical questions such as 'Have you been concerned your blood looks more like Ribena than the finest Merlot?' help to engage the reader in a fun and everyday way. The use of 'finest Merlot' when talking about blood also introduces a sense of humour. Although the language contains lots of technical terms such as 'haemoglobin', these do not make the piece off-putting as the rest uses everyday language.

The whole article is presented in an accessible way. The columns break the writing up and the eye is drawn to the pictures and information in boxes. Once you have read that you are more likely to read the whole article.
(5 marks)

6 Platelets help to clot blood. If your blood doesn't clot you won't stop bleeding when you get cut.
(1 mark)

7a The headings help to break the information up into chunks that are easy to read and learn.
(1 mark)

7b The bullet points help students to learn the information. This is a textbook, so the information needs to be very clear and obvious. Students don't have time to pick information out from long paragraphs.
(1 mark)

8a and b *You might have provided any of these answers:*
- (microbes) This gives a technical name for the organisms. Students can still understand the sentence even if they don't know the technical name.
- (blood proteins) These brackets provide more detail about the other chemicals in the blood.
- (slightly yellow) These brackets provide more detail about the 'almost colourless liquid'. The extra detail might help a student to remember it.
- (glucose, amino acids, fats) These brackets provide detail and specific examples of what the dissolved food is made up of.
- (carbon dioxide, urea) These brackets provide more detail about the waste products in plasma.
- (about 95 000 km) This provides the specific detail about the distance around the Earth.

(1 mark for the information in brackets and its explanation)

9 *You might have one of the following ideas:*
This text has been written to:
- help students to learn about blood.
- explain about blood.
- provide information about what blood is made up of.
(1 mark)

10 The extract makes the topic easy for the reader to follow by the use of layout and the general structure of the information. For example, sub-headings such as 'Red blood cells' and 'White blood cells' make it really clear what the paragraph is going to be about. This helps the reader to navigate as s/he can scan the text to find the section s/he needs. The pictures also help as they are really clear and link directly to the text – they illustrate it. Bullet points also help to break the text into easily manageable pieces.

The language is very technical because this is a technical subject. However, many technical terms are put into brackets so that the student can follow the text without them, or they are explained clearly, for example 'plasma'. On the whole the language is clear and simple, which means the reader is not going to be put off completely. Even if s/he doesn't understand the technical term it is likely they will be able to work it out. There are a lot of numbers in this extract, especially in the final paragraph. These give the piece credibility and make it seem more factual.

The piece is structured with many simple or compound sentences, mostly pretty short. This is because it needs to explain its knowledge quickly and clearly. It is not about revealing the interesting information with tension and suspense – it is about making it fast and clear.
(5 marks)

11 *You might have one of the following:*
- Watson thinks Holmes is clever. We know this because he asks how he knows about Afghanistan 'in astonishment'.
- Watson thinks Holmes is dedicated to his studies. We know this because he calls him a 'student … absorbed in his work'.
- Watson thinks Holmes gets very excited about things. We know this because he describes him as 'delighted as a child with a new toy'.
(2 marks: 1 for the idea and 1 for the quotation/evidence)

12 Holmes claims his idea is important because it will help apply justice and find out if a mark on the clothes of a suspect is blood or not.
(1 mark)

13 The writer has used alliteration of 'l' in 'lofty', 'lined' and 'littered' to make the room seem really big. The phrase 'lined and littered' emphasises the fact that it is full of scientific equipment. The sight seems almost overwhelming and this is supported by the word 'countless'.
(2 marks)

14 Sherlock Holmes is made to seem like someone fixated on an obsession in this extract. At first the whole room has been given over to his experiment; you can't even count the bottles of chemicals. Holmes is 'absorbed' and bent over the table – this makes him seem really obsessed.

However, when people enter the room he is excited and gives 'a cry of pleasure' which makes him seem more human. However, all he wants to do is show off his powers of deduction and the result of his experiment. This makes him seem quite selfish – he doesn't ask why they have come to visit, he just says, 'The question now is about haemoglobin'.

Finally, my impression is of someone who actually wants glory as well as justice as he names the test after himself – 'The Sherlock Holmes test'! He thinks he has made a great breakthrough for the world and is really pleased with himself. Overall, my impression is of someone who is self-interested and clever.
(5 marks)

Writing answers

pages 138–139

1

Text	Intended audience	Purpose
1	Local council members	Inform, describe, persuade
2	Your whole year group	Persuade, argue
3	Head teacher	Persuade, argue
4	Potential customer (head teacher)	Persuade, inform, explain
5	Project manager	Advise, review

2 Level 5 (mid)

Bridge School
Bridge Lane
Liverpool
L13 7DG

Dear Premium Cycle

I am writing to complain about the cycle sheds you sold our school last year because they are falling to pieces. You said they were 'long lasting and guaranteed for ten years' however this is obviously not true as there is extensive rust to the sides

Schools don't have much money so I think it's not really fair you should sell us a bad product. The students are the ones who are missing out because the money that will be spent to repair the product should have been spent on new books.

We want to claim on the guarantee so please send me details of how to do so; this will help to make me believe in your company again. It would be even better if you were to build us a new shed free of charge. We will make sure the local paper has a photo of this which would be good publicity for you

Yours sincerley,
Tim Potter

This is level 5 because:

Sentence structure, punctuation and text organisation
- **Set out as a formal letter, including an address**, greeting and sign-off (although the name of the company is wrong and 'sincerely' is spelt incorrectly!)
- **Some range in sentence structures** and they are starting to be used for effect.
- **Clear paragraphing.**
- **A semi-colon** has been used to make a complex sentence.
- **Connectives** such as 'however' and 'which' are used.

Composition and effect
- **Language and layout just about matches the audience and purpose** – perhaps a little immature in its tone.

Spelling
- **Simple and common polysyllabic words spelt accurately** (except 'sincerely', which is a really common error).

3 Purpose = advise
Audience = radio controller
Text type = report

pages 140–141

1

negative	neutral	positive
dull	ordinary	stimulating
boring	normal	essential
tedious	necessary	exciting
mundane	commonplace	interesting
dull	usual	vital
wearisome		crucial
monotonous		

'Challenging' could be used in a positive or a negative way!

2 *There are lots of verbs available, for example:*

a go: move, proceed, depart, journey, travel, advance

b said: cried, shouted, mumbled, whispered, sobbed, pronounced

c sleep: doze, slumber, nap, snooze, rest, drowse

d cry: sob, wail, weep, bawl, howl, snivel

e walk: stroll, saunter, plod, trudge, stride, march

3 *Here are some you might have thought of:*

a This product is really *excellent / top class / first class / exceptional*.

b I'll *talk to / call / meet* you later.

c I *am not sure / don't know / am undecided* as to what to suggest.

d *Hello / Good morning / Good evening / Good afternoon*.

e We don't want to be *overcharged / given a bad deal*.

4 *Here are some possible similes:*

a a really fierce deputy headteacher: as fierce as a bulldog

b a jolly and cheerful football coach: like a beach ball on a sunny day

c a huge grey factory: like a field of concrete

d a small boat out at sea: as vulnerable as a butterfly

e a child skiing down a mountain: like a fearless cannonball

5 *For example:*

a Yob attacks grandmother.

b The Guildford Flames slaughtered their opposition.

c When the sun is blazing a cold drink tastes wonderful.

d We are trapped inside the house by blankets of snow.

e The ancient cat attempted to catch a bird and failed.

6 *For example:*

a The man was attacked by the bear.

b The woodland was damaged by a fire.

c He quickly ate his burger.

d She cried out as the young man took her handbag.

e The old school buildings could be dangerous.

pages 142–143

1a I am very excited because I am going on holiday to America tomorrow! My whole family are going; what's really good is that I am allowed to take my best friend.

1b Cats are natural predators; when they see a bird or mouse it just means excitement to them. Sometimes they kill without the desire to eat their prey or can be shocked when they catch something.

2a The market was full of exciting smells, colours, noises, people and new things.

2b Music can create the atmosphere you need to learn; it can even help you to remember ideas. When you come to revise you can listen to the same music and it will help you to recall the original idea; your memory will have made a link.

3 *There are lots of possible answers. Here are some examples:*

a At the end of the garden, beyond the tree, was the silent lake.

b In the car, sitting quietly as directed, the boy watched the events unfold.

c In the corner of the room, hidden by the shadows, crouched the murderer.

d Under the floorboards, in a dusty envelope, was the secret plan.

4 *In answers a–c, the main clauses are underlined and the subordinate clauses are in italics.*

a <u>I hid under the duvet shaking,</u> *as the storm raged outside.*

b <u>Claire,</u> *who was filled with a sense of relief,* <u>left the stage.</u>

c *Until the power cut hit,* <u>Paul refused to leave his computer.</u>

Here are three possible answers for d–f:

d Sally loved the book; she missed her bus because she was reading it.
Sally, who missed a bus because she was reading, loved the book.
Even though she missed her bus, Sally loved the book.

e The computer finally died; it had been used non-stop.

11

The computer, which had been used non-stop, finally died.

Due to its non-stop use, the computer finally died.

f Amanda bought some new pink shoes; she loved shopping.

Amanda, who loved shopping, bought some new pink shoes.

Loving shopping, Amanda bought some new pink shoes.

pages 144–145

1 When you first see my house you might think it's a bit dull and dingy because there are plants growing up the front wall and the path is a bit overgrown. I like to think this adds character and makes it more exciting when you come and visit me.

Stepping through the front door for the first time is normally a bit of a shock because we've painted the inside really bright colours. The woodwork (that's the doors and skirting boards) is pink and the walls are purple. My gran hates it, but we sat down and made a family decision so it's fine by us.

Once you are in you'll probably be drawn into the kitchen as there's generally something good cooking and that's where we tend to be. It's funny really, as it's the smallest room in the house but it's where we spend our time together. (Well, not the smallest, but you wouldn't all sit round the bathroom to talk about the day, would you?)

If I trust you, and the others say it's OK, I might take you to the end of the garden to see our den. It's taken us years to create it and it's simply the best place to be in the summer.

2 "Look, I'm really sorry," said Barry with frustration, "but this is just not going to work and that's an end to it." He threw down the play script and stood up to go.

Laura looked up at him, "I'm really sorry as well," she said with sarcasm, "I'm really sorry that we've wasted so much time rehearsing with you in the lead role when we could have had Lance. He would at least have listened to our ideas."

"That's just typical," replied Barry, "and that's why I'm leaving. You've never wanted me in this stupid play. Well, if you think Lance will have anything to do with you when he hears how you've treated me you've got another think coming!"

The rest of the cast sat watching with amazement as he coolly collected his jacket and walked out of the rehearsal room. Laura sat stunned.

"Did that really just happen?" she asked, "Did we finally get rid of that idiot?"

"Yes!" shouted Sian with joy, "Well done, you finally did it!"

3 *Firstly*, pre-heat the oven to 180°.

Secondly, take your vegetables and chop them into 1cm size cubes.

Then lightly oil the baking tray and arrange the vegetables on it so they are evenly spaced.

Next put the tray in the oven and set the timer to 40 minutes.

Finally remove the vegetables from the oven and enjoy!

pages 146–147

1 • Your address in the top right: *letter*

• Impersonal phrases: *report*

• The date: *letter, newspaper story*

• Snappy headline: *newspaper story*

• Alliteration: *letter, newspaper story, leaflet, speech*

• Short paragraphs: *newspaper story, leaflet, report*

• Bullet points: *leaflet, report*

• Sign off of 'Yours faithfully, Yours sincerely' or a more informal phrase if you know the person: *letter*

• Rhetorical techniques: *letter, newspaper story, leaflet, speech*

• Entertain and inform: *letter, newspaper story, speech*

• Informal style: *letter*

• Repetition: *letter, newspaper story, leaflet, speech*

• Clear but lively: *speech*

• Factual: *report*

• Formal address: *report*

• Short sentences: *newspaper story, report*

• Clear statement of purpose: *report*

• Sub-heading: *newspaper story, leaflet*

• Modal verbs: *leaflet, report, speech*

• Emotive language: *letter, newspaper story, leaflet, speech*

• Personal pronouns: *letter, leaflet, speech*

• The address of the person you are writing to in the top left: *letter*

• Formal style: *letter, newspaper story, leaflet, report, speech*

- Quotations from experts: *newspaper story, speech*

- Pattern of three: *newspaper story, leaflet, speech*

- Varied length of sentences: *letter, leaflet, speech*

2

headline   *sub-heading*

PET FISH FRIED
Fish lover left red-faced

Paul Roberts, fish owning expert, was left red-faced yesterday, after he managed to fry hundreds of pounds worth of Koi Carp.

Roberts, who travels the world advising on the care of these creatures, fitted his own water filter system, something he advises his readers to leave to the professionals.

Unfortunately, he made a fatal error with the wiring and managed to heat his pond to near-tropical temperatures! The poor fish didn't stand a chance, as their home boiled and then exploded.

The stone pond exploded under the pressure of the boiling water and the boiled carp were sent flying. "My cat thought it was wonderful as cooked fish came flying through the air" explained Roberts' neighbour, Brian Downing, "although it was a horrendous noise!"

Roberts wasn't available for comment, but his wife said he was shocked and very saddened.

£400 Koi cat food

caption   *illustration*

3

alliteration

" Everybody knows that litter is <u>dirty and dangerous</u>. <u>So why do we just drop our litter?</u>

repetition

Rats are attracted to places with lots of litter, such as our school. Now, you might have an idea of rats as <u>cute and cuddly</u>, but they actually spread <u>dangerous diseases</u> such as <u>cholera, typhus and leptospirosis</u>. We do not want these around our school, <u>so why do we just drop our litter?</u>

alliteration
list of three

<u>We need to make a stand. We need to make a difference. You need to make a difference.</u>

repetition/ list of three

Firstly, take responsibility for your own actions. Put your litter in a bin or your bag.

Secondly, take responsibility for our community. Challenge anyone you see dropping litter. Explain what the consequences could be and ask them to put their litter in a bin.

Finally, if you see a piece of litter, <u>don't walk over it: deal with it.</u> By doing this you will <u>make a difference</u>."

emotive language

repetition

pages 148–149

1 **a** I am going to the shop to buy some crisps and my dog needs to walk.

b The shopping centre banned teenagers as they were bad news, they thought.

c James and Amanda are going to France to learn to ski; I hope they enjoy it.

d I can't believe Top of the Pops is still going after all these years; it's really amazing.

e My English teacher is going to be really impressed with my improved writing skills.

2 **a** You will need a pen, a pencil and a ruler.

b I had a great birthday, thanks.
OR I had a great birthday – thanks.

c Jane likes Shakespeare; Caroline prefers modern drama.

d The bread (which was actually put out for the birds) had been eaten by the cat.
OR The bread, which was actually put out for the birds, had been eaten by the cat.
OR The bread – which was actually put out for the birds – had been eaten by the cat.

3 **a** I'm **b** it's **c** they're **d** you're **e** we're

4 **a** he is **b** let us **c** could have **d** can not
e we have

5 **a** Lucy's cats were hungry.

b Let's all go round to Wayne's flat for a party.

c I won all the prizes at my school's sports day.

d My town's provision for young people is inadequate.

e My brother's car is a heap of junk.

pages 150–151

1 **a** buses **b** tries **c** potatoes **d** churches
e children **f** sheep **g** foxes **h** cars
i tomatoes **j** businesses **k** calves **l** rushes

2

a	to run	running	ran
b	to stop	stopping	stopped
c	to drop	dropping	dropped
d	to decide	deciding	decided
e	to watch	watching	watched
f	to form	forming	formed
g	to admit	admitting	admitted
h	to prefer	preferring	preferred
i	to benefit	benefiting	benefited
j	to state	stating	stated
k	to fight	fighting	fought
l	to begin	beginning	began

3 **a** accommodation **g** interesting
b assessment **h** marriage
c audience **i** people
d business **j** receive
e embarrass **k** secondary
f explanation **l** separate

m sincerely **o** tomorrow
n surprise **p** weird

4 **a** Lance and Susan are looking forward to *their* holiday.

b "*Whose* homework is this?" asked the teacher. "It doesn't have a name!"

c The old house was very creepy at night because it was so *quiet*.

d "You may all go to lunch *except* Katie."

e You need to explain the *effect* of the metaphor.

f Oh, look! My pen is over *there*.

g "*Who's* up for swimming?" asked Andrea.

h I was *quite* pleased with my homework but the teacher didn't seem impressed.

i I've got to go up in assembly to *accept* a prize on behalf of my tutor group.

page 152   Level 5 (mid)

Hi Luke,

Thanks for your email, there's a book I've really enjoyed and I think you will as well.

The book is the first Alex Rider book and it's called 'Stormbreaker'; it's really good. It's about a boy called Alex Rider, surprisingly enough. It's got a really good start, all about when the doorbell rings in the middle of the night it means something bad has happened, which is true when you think about it.

Anyway, Alex has lots of adventures and he's a bit like James bond cos he's got loads of gagets like a gameboy that is also a bug detecter which is cool.

I really like Alex and I think I'd like to be a spy when I'm older – but he's a spy at our age. It'd be really cool as you've got the gagets and can do whatever you like and the security services just cover it up and you get away with it.

In conclusion, you'll like this book because it's exciting, it's original and it's about someone who's just like us. Read it!

See you soon,

Sebastian

This is level 5 because:

Sentence structure, punctuation and text organisation

• **Some range in sentence structures** – it uses complex sentences to control the writing and show relationships between ideas.

• **Clear paragraphing** helps the reader follow the line of argument.

• **Some complex sentences** – these make the ideas seem more complex.

• **Good use of connectives** such as 'Anyway' and 'In conclusion'. These help the reader to follow the line of argument and make the writing flow well.

- **The ending is well crafted.** The pattern of three – 'it's exciting, it's original and it's about someone who's just like us' – provides a strong conclusion to the whole piece. The pattern of three is a traditional technique that is often very powerful.

Composition and effect

- **Tone appropriate for the purpose.** This means the writing is just right for an email from one teenager to another in a formal setting. Remember you are really writing for the examiner!
- **Clear viewpoint supported by evidence.** Sebastian is very clear about his reasons for recommending this book. He provides evidence to support his ideas and this makes us more likely to believe him.
- **Suits the audience** – the sign-off 'see you soon' is a good example.

Spelling

- **Simple and common polysyllabic words spelt accurately.** 'Polysyllabic' means 'more than one syllable' and refers to words Sebastian has spelt correctly such as 'surprisingly' and 'conclusion'. His spelling isn't perfect, however, and he does spell more difficult words such as 'gadgets' and 'detector' incorrectly. This is part of the reason he stays on level 5.

page 153 — Level 5 (mid)

Uniform survey

The students were asked what they wanted to do about uniform and all but 20% said they wanted a new uniform. Therefore we need a new uniform.

The girls want to wear trousers, but not the really nasty pleated trousers, they want nice ones (they don't have to be to fashionable). The boys want to be able to wear trainers (they'll wear black ones as they look like shoes but are more comfortable).

What you should do now

You should ask a group of students to do some designs for a smart uniform and let the students vote on what they want. This would be good because it's letting the students decide what they want and if they pick a smart uniform then they'll wear it.

When you've got the results you can check it is not too fashionable and is good to work in.

Different uniform for GCSE

It's a good idea to have a different uniform for GCSE to show they are at the top of the school and this gives them more status. This will make them more responsible. Also, they don't wear uniform properly at the moment, so this might make them do that.

This is level 5 because:

Sentence structure, punctuation and text organisation

- **Clear structure** – the sub-headings are a really good idea as they help to structure the response.
- **Comments supported by evidence**, such as 'This would be good because …' . This shows thought and means the comments have more substance.
- **Some noun phrases** such as 'the really nasty pleated trousers' help to add relevant detail and make the commentary come to life.

Composition and effect

- **Suitable level of formality.** The structure and language is correct for the purpose and audience.
- **Clear viewpoint supported by evidence.** This commentary provides a clear answer for the Leadership Team. The evidence gives it authority.
- **Appropriate stylistic features** such as the sub-headings make this response work.

Spelling

- **Usually accurate although some careless errors** such as the misspelling of 'survey' in the heading. This is careless because it is a word that was used on the question itself!

page 154 — Level 5 (low)

My great-granmother is really interesting because she was in the war and she's got really interesting stories about the things that she did.

She was a taxi-driver and used to drive all the solders around and make sure they were in the right place. It was really unusual for a woman to do these things and she never stopped wearing trousers afterwards. She hated the food but she loved going to dances and being able to drive around all the time.

This has affected her today because she is still really strong, except for her legs which don't work, and she still says what she thinks and makes her views known. She says the war was really good for women as it stopped her doing boring stuff. Other people in her nursing home get upset when she says this but I think it's cool that she thinks this, even if I don't like war.

I think she's a strong and fasinating woman; I hope to be as strong as her when I'm her age.

This is level 5 because:

Sentence structure, punctuation and text organisation
- **Range in sentence structures supports the comments.** The semi-colon in the final paragraph links the ideas together.
- **Clear paragraphing and development of ideas.** The reader can easily follow the description.
- **Some punctuation within complex sentences.** This punctuation helps the reader to follow ideas.

Composition and effect
- **Clear viewpoint supported by evidence.** This gives credibility to the description and helps it come to life.
- **Appropriate stylistic features**, such as the use of evidence and reported opinions.
- **Other viewpoints recognised.** This makes the piece more sophisticated and balanced.

Spelling
- **Mostly correct.**

page 155   Level 5 (mid)

This holiday sounds really good and I think we should go on it.

Mum will love the relaxation zone and will be able to sooth away the stress she always moans about. She can get beauty tips and gossipe with other mums who will also be there.

Mark can just play his gutare all week. That's what he'd do wherever we go, so it'll be fine for him. I know he says he hates organised music, but this could be really exciting and different.

I can learn to dive and windsurf which'll be really cool. I really want to explore what's under the sea and you know it'll mean I'm doing it safely – which is what counts, really.

I think this'll be fun for all of us and we can meet up to eat together in the evenings and then we'll have something to talk about and we might actually talk rather than shout at Mark for playing his gutare all the time.

This could be just the thing our family needs: a chance to do what we all like doing without anyone feeling stressed that they're having a bad time. I think this could be the holiday of our dreams. Lets go!

This is level 5 because:

Sentence structure, punctuation and text organisation
- **Contains a range of sentence structures** and supports ideas with reasons. These help the explanation.
- **Clear paragraphing and development of ideas** help the reader to follow the explanation.

- **Some punctuation within sentences/complex sentences.** However, some of them get out of control, e.g. the second to last paragraph. This needs to be split into shorter sentences with a range of punctuation.

Composition and effect
- **Clear viewpoint supported by evidence.** This gives the explanation more authority.
- **Appropriate stylistic features**, such as the use of connectives to persuade: 'I know he hates organised music, but this could be really exciting and different.' These support the purpose.
- **Recognises other's viewpoints** and addresses them, making the answer more sophisticated.

Spelling
- **Mostly correct.**

page 156   Level 5 (mid)

"I can't believe it's finally upon us, " Ann said with enthusiasm, "let's get going!" She turned to her fellow space travellers as there spaceship landed on the planet and the dust settled. She wasn't shocked to see Mark looking worried as usual.

"We need to test and check the area again." Mark said with his usual caution.

"You are so predictable" Afsheet cried "just follow every rule twice and then you might consider it. Just remember why we are here!"

They looked at each other and slowly smiled. Although Mark was a nervous and double-checking sort of person he knew he wanted to see what was on Planet X but he also knew it was the most dangerous thing any human being had ever done. Ever. It was exciting to be one of the bravest of the human race.

The instruments beeped, "Beep" and they all smiled again. "That's the all clear" said Ann.

The door beeped twice, "beep beep" and Afsheen turned to the others with anticipation, "Well?" he asked.

"DO IT!" they shouted; the door hissed and opened to the new planet.

This is level 5 because:

Sentence structure and punctuation
- **Variety of sentence structures**, which gives the piece more interest.
- **Connectives clarify the narrative sequence** and help the reader follow the events.
- **Range of punctuation**, mostly used accurately.

Text structure and organisation

- **Detail used to develop ideas.** This makes the story more interesting.
- **Paragraphs sequenced effectively.** These help the story to flow and allow the reader to follow the events.
- **Connectives** such as 'Although' are used to make the narrative coherent. This means they help the story to flow in a way that makes sense.

Composition and effect

- **Narrative voice used to develop character and plot.** The narration helps the reader to understand the characters and the events.
- **Narrative viewpoint controlled** to present clear view of characters and plot.
- **Effective choice of vocabulary.**

page 158　Level 5 (high)

My town

My town is just one of those ordinary, sleepy, rather boring places that can be found everywhere. It's between two bigger towns so no-one really comes here, it's just a place to live, and hang out if no-one stops you.

Local life

If you are into growing marows or making your own wine there's loads to do as that's all people seem to do round here. My mum actually went to a local history talk the other day about some guy who used to live here. (That was quite good though as I then had my mates round.) There are things to do if you're younger as well like music clubs and nusery. It's just it's a bit slow for the teenagers.

The best bits

The best bits are the woods and lake where we've been going for years and now have some cool places to sit. But if you're older you'll like the town. There are places for kids like plate painting and the sports centre does a Saturday morning club, but that's really for kids not teenagers.

Things that need to be changed

Basically, as you've probably guessed, we need more things for teenagers to do. At the moment we just go round each other's houses and play the computer or watch tv. That's fine, but there really should be something for us. Lots of people would like a skate ramp and even the skaters would go there to hang out, so that would be a good thing.

My overall impression

Well, what do you think? Overall my town is ok; it's great if you're a young kid or an adult, but not so good if you're a teenager. That makes it ok overall.

This is level 5 because:

Sentence structure and punctuation

- **Variety of sentence structures**, which makes the writing more interesting and helps the writer to say exactly what they mean.
- **Embedded subordinate clauses**, such as 'as you've probably guessed', help to engage the reader by addressing them directly.
- **Range of punctuation**, mostly accurate. This includes commas, apostrophes and brackets.

Text structure and organisation

- **Detail used to develop ideas.** This helps the reader to understand what is being described.
- **Paragraphs well sequenced.** Sub-headings help the reader to navigate the description and understand how the line of thought develops. The piece develops logically.

Composition and effect

- **Clear voice** engages and sustains reader's interest. Although the piece has some informal moments, e.g. when it gives personal stories, it doesn't bring the piece down too much because the task did ask for personal opinions.
- **Rhetorical question**, 'Well, what do you think?' helps sustain reader's interest and asks them to actively think about the content of the description.
- **Good choice of vocabulary.** It isn't complex, but it is appropriate for the task. If it were more complex it would help the piece to improve.

page 160　Level 5 (high)

Dear Aunty Margaret

Thank you for your letter, I've just done my options choices at school so that's been the biggest thing to happen, really. In fact, it's made me feel really grown up – I can't believe I've just made choices about my future – I'm thirteen for goodness sake; far too young for that sort of thing.

Right, so what have I chosen? Well, you don't actually get that much of a choice as there's so many you HAVE to do (English, maths, science, German) for starters. I've gone for geography as I've always liked that and the teacher's really cool, then I've picked music (shouldn't be too difficult as I play the piano), graphics and electronics. Electronics is new to me, but it sounds good and Mr Dinning's really fun and everyone really likes him.

It's really difficult though, I don't have a clue what I want to do when I leave school (well, I hope to go to university and have fun for three years like Matt did!!) It sort of seems wrong that we have to make these decisions now, although I'm really pleased I don't have to do drama ever again (that's just such an embarrassing lesson).

Is it really that different from when you were at school? I bet not. Well, I'm pretty sure you didn't do electronics, but the English, maths, science etc etc must be the same.

Right, time to do my homework, see you when we visit in the summer!

Bye for now!

Alex

This is level 5 because:

Sentence structure and punctuation
- **Variety of sentence structures.** This helps to shape the piece and make it more interesting to read.
- **Dashes and brackets used appropriately.**
- **Range of punctuation**, mostly used accurately.

Text structure and organisation
- **Detail used to develop ideas.** This helps the reader to follow and understand the letter.
- **Paragraphs well sequenced.** A new paragraph is started for each new shift in topic. This helps the reader follow the information.
- **Connectives**, such as 'although' and 'Right,' are used to lead the reader through the piece.

Composition and effect
- **Clear voice** engages and sustains reader's interest. This is a letter to a relative so the chatty tone and structure is appropriate.
- **Bracketed asides**, e.g. '(Well, I hope to go to university and have fun for three years like Matt did!!),' bring the letter to life and add character.

page 162 · Level 5 (high)

Music Wrap

The great new gadget that's going to change the world.

This job is great sometimes as I'm able to get my hands on the new best gadget before it hits the shops. Today was one of those days and I'm so excited about this new music player.

The thing that makes it special is it doesn't look like a music player: it looks like a watch! (although it is a bit chunky)

This watch does everything you'd want from a watch like telling the time, but it is also a music player. Yes, you can download your mp3s and play them from this music watch.

Yeah, but then I've got to trail a wire up my sleeve, I hear you cry! Well, no, you don't, because the

headphones for this beauty are wireless!!! Yes, two great new inventions in one! Just tuck the phones into your ears, select your track, press play and there you have it: music in your ears!

Pros: You can't lose it, it's always with you, no-one knows you're listening to music.

Cons: the watch is a bit chunky (but this is just the first release). It could be easy to lose the headphones.

Overall rating: FANTASTIC GO GET ONE TODAY!

This is level 5 because:

Sentence structure and punctuation
- **Variety of sentence structures** makes the writing more interesting and controls the ideas.
- **Dashes and brackets used appropriately.**
- **Range of punctuation**, mostly used accurately. However, speech marks are missing for, 'Yeah, but then I've got to trail a wire up my sleeve'.

Text structure and organisation
- **Detail used to develop ideas.** The detail about the job provides a context which helps us understand how much value to place on this review. It makes the writer appear to be an expert – exactly the person we'd want to review a product.
- **Paragraphs sequenced effectively.** Each paragraph moves the review on with a new aspect of the product.
- **Final section appropriate** ('Pros', 'Cons' and 'Overall rating') for a review. It helps to shape the answer effectively.

Composition and effect
- **Clear voice** engages and sustains reader's interest.
- **Appropriate for purpose and audience.** This is clearly a review rather than an advertisement or personal response, both forms of writing that students might be tempted to produce.

page 164 · Level 5 (high)

Dear Mr Planning Officer

I am writing to make my objections to the supermarket being built on the skatepark known.

My reasons are as follows:

Firstly, we need the skate park as a creative and safe place for the teenagers of this town to go. Many towns have problems with their teenagers having nothing to do: we don't have those problems and that's mainly due to the skatepark.

Secondly, the teenagers of this town raised the money for that park to be built. My brother did loads of sponsored events and collected £100s of pounds towards it. Are you now saying his really hard work was wasted as you're just going to give the land away? That's not fair!

Finally, do we really need another huge supermarket? The town has got three of these already and surely that's enough? How many of these places do we really need? We've got three big supermarkets and lots of little local shops; these might go out of business if you let the supermarket change our town for the worst.

Thank you for listening to my views, I am sure you will make the right decision and NOT let the supermarket destroy our town.

Yours faithfully,

Jane Cutler

This is level 5 because:

Sentence structure and punctuation
- **Variety of sentence structures**, including complex sentences, e.g. 'Many towns have problems with their teenagers having nothing to do: we don't have those problems and that's mainly due to the skatepark'.
- **Range of punctuation**, mostly used accurately.
- **Ideas linked by a range of devices**, such as connectives and punctuation.

Text structure and organisation
- **Detail used to develop ideas.** Detail really helps a piece of writing to live in the mind of the reader.
- **Paragraphs sequenced effectively** and the use of connectives such as 'firstly', 'secondly' and 'finally' really helps lead the reader through the letter.

Composition and effect
- **Clear voice** engages and sustains reader's interest. It appears balanced as it considers other points of view, but when you read carefully it is very much in favour of the skatepark.
- **Good use of rhetorical questions.**
- **Appropriate for purpose and audience.** This 'advice' is very one-sided, but gives the impression of considering both sides of the situation.

page 168 Level 5 (mid)

Dear Governors,

Thank you for the opportunity to explain my point of view on this very important subject; it is good to know that the students have a voice in this school.

Deciding how to spend this generous gift is a responsibility, but everyone knows that the school's sports facilities are in need of improvement. Sports is essential for a healthy life, and experts have conducted many studies where they have shown sport helps you to study and keep fit. Therefore, I suggest we spend the money on sports equipment.

I conducted a survey of Year 9 students, remember, these students are in the middle of their school time and so know what the school needs, and will be able to benefit from any purchase. They all said sports stuff was needed. Lots of the boys want it to be spent on football and cricket and the girls said a swimming pool. Maybe we should split the money and have a swimming pool and more football stuff. That would keep everyone happy.

Swimming is an essential skill. If you can swim your chances of drowning are reduced (although you can drown in 5 cms of water). Therefore, I think we should buy a swimming pool. Who knows how many lives this might save?

I look forward to the pool opening,

Thanks for listening!

Sally Archer

This is level 5 because:

Sentence structure and punctuation
- **Variety of sentence structures**, including complex sentences such as the first one.
- **Range of punctuation, mostly used accurately.** This shows the student is really trying to control and manipulate the language to support her ideas.
- **Connectives**, such as 'Therefore,' are used within paragraphs to develop ideas. They show the relationship between the survey and the recommendation, so are very powerful.

Text structure and organisation
- **Detail used to develop ideas.**
- **Paragraphs generally well sequenced**, although there is a feeling that the ideas change as the writing continues. If the student had planned more carefully she might not have made this error. It is a major one, and is a key factor in preventing her getting a higher level.

Composition and effect
- **Clear voice** engages and sustains reader's interest.
- **Good use of rhetorical question** 'Who knows how many lives this might save?'.
- **Mostly appropriate for purpose and audience** but it could be more formal considering the audience.

19

page 170 Level 5 (mid)

Ideas for new Teen TV Show

The research shows teenagers want people their own age, or slightly older. This is key to developping this new show. It needs to be fast, fun and furious and that'll pull in the viewers.

The presenters

We need late teenage/early 20s presenters and they've got to be good looking. A boy and a girl will attract boys and girls watching. They should be fasionable and funny, and not talk down to the viewers as if they're stupid or young.

The show

The show needs to be a magazine show; this means like a magazine that you can dip into and nothing goes on too long to get bored, but it's not all fast and crash/bang.

There should be a good band on every week, not just the sad soap star who wants a pop carer, but proper bands who are at the top of the charts (maybe the download charts as there more realistic?)

Everyone likes adventure sports, so there could be something on them.

This show's going to be great!

This is level 5 because:

Sentence structure, punctuation and text organisation
- **Range in sentence structures**, including complex sentences such as the third paragraph.
- **Clear paragraphing and development.** The ideas are structured to allow the reader to follow them. The paragraphs also move the ideas on in a logical way. The sub-headings help this.

Composition and effect
- **Clear viewpoint supported by evidence.**
- **Appropriate stylistic features**, such as the sub-headings, support the purpose.
- **Answer focused on the task.**

Spelling
- **Mostly correct**, but errors in words such as 'fashionable' and 'developing'.

Shakespeare answers

The Tempest
page 176

1 1C, 2D, 3A, 4B

2

Quotation	Technique	Effect
'the wild waves whist'	alliteration of 'w'	Reflects the movement of the waves and spray
'the fringèd curtains of thine eye'	Metaphor – her eyelids are curtains and the lashes a fringe to the curtains	Reminds us that Prospero can send Miranda to sleep at will due to his magic and her eyes are key to her understanding the world. This metaphor now also has a modern meaning as theatres often have curtains that raise for the action
'thou shalt be as free As mountain winds'	Simile comparing freedom with how the mountain winds move	We remember that the mountain winds can go anywhere and everywhere and cannot be controlled – this is the freedom Ariel longs for
'But you – o you, So perfect and so peerless – are created Of every creature's best'	Alliteration of 'p' and 'c'	The repeated sounds link the words together and build up their strength

pages 178–179

What impression do you get of Miranda in these scenes?

Level 4 (low)

Miranda is just manipulated by her father to fall in love with Ferdinand in these scenes. She falls in love with Ferdinand because he is the first man she's seen (after her father and Caliban). This is what Prospero wants because he tells her that Ferdinand is good-looking, 'gallant' and 'goody person' this means he is noble, which is good and people think he is good-looking. Miranda straightaway says Ferdinand is 'a thing divine'.

She is also quite in your face as she starts talking about being a virgin and she basically proposes to Ferdinand which isn't how women were meant to behave back then.

It's the first time she has argued with her dad but he makes her do this and it's meant to show that she is changing and growing up because she argues with him.

All the stuff about carrying logs is just a way to get them to say they love each other and Miranda is up front with how she feels and talks about being a virgin – 'my modesty the jewel in my dower' – which you just don't do, especially when you've just been on an island with a monster and your dad. This shows Miranda doesn't really know how to behave or what people do or don't say but it has the right effect and she proposes to Ferdinand who also proposes to her.

The impression I get of her is a girl who is manipulated but then says what she wants. And gets it.

This is level 4 because:

- It shows good personal understanding of Miranda and her situation.

- It covers both scenes and identifies some relevant points.

- It links the text to the social, cultural and historic context.

- It is too narrative – it tells the story rather than analysing the characters.

- It uses quotations but these are not explained fully.

To raise the level the student needs to:

- Provide more quotations and explain them fully – what they show us of the characters and themes.

- Provide some explanation of the language and its effects.

- Make sure the question is answered fully throughout the answer – this student just remembers about it at the end of the answer.

What impression do you get of Ferdinand in these scenes?

Level 4 (low)

My impression of Ferdinand is a man who falls in love in these scenes. He starts by thinking his father and everyone is dead, 'my drowned father'. And then he sees Miranda and falls in love. He thinks she's a goddess, 'more like the goddess on whom these airs attend' but asks if she's a maid or not, 'are you a maid or no?' This means are you human or a goddess but it also means are you a virgin because this was really important in those times.

He tells them he's now the King of Naples and says he'll marry Miranda, 'I'll make you the Queen of Naples' but then Prospero interferes and gets nasty and uses his magic so Ferdinand can't move. Ferdinand is really confused, which is fair enough, 'my spirits as in a dream are all bound up. My father's loss, the weakness which I feel, The wreck of all my friends, not this man's threats, to whom I am subdued, are but light to me.'

We do feel really sorry for him. He has just lost his dad and is stuck on this island. Suddenly this beautiful woman appears. It must all be a bit much.

In the next scene he is moving logs for Prospero and Miranda comes to talk to him and they agree they love each other and will get married so he is happy even though he is moving logs, 'I this patient log-man'.

So my impression of Ferdinand is of a man who is upset and confused but then falls in love.

This is level 4 because:

- It shows understanding of what happens in these scenes.

- It tries to answer the question at the start and end of the answer.

- It is too narrative – it tells the story rather than analysing it.

- It uses some quotations but these are not explained and one is far too long. They are also not all accurate.

To raise the level the student needs to:

- Turn the answer from narrative to analysis and explanation.

- Use quotations to support the ideas and provide explanation about them and what they show us of the character.

- Provide some comment and explanation of the language and its effects.

page 180

How is the theme of love explored in these scenes?

Level 4 (low)

This play shows that love can be really fast and that it will make you do things you wouldn't normally do like move logs or go against your father.

Miranda is really in love with Ferdinand as she calls him a thing divine, 'a thing divine, for nothing natural I ever saw so noble'. This shows us that she thinks he's divine.

Ferdinand is really in love with Miranda as he calls her a goddess, 'most sure the goddess on whom these airs attend'. This shows us that he thinks she's a goddess.

Miranda loves Ferdinand so much that she goes against her father (Prospero), 'Beseech you father', and she hangs onto his garments to try and stop him. She also talks to Ferdinand when he is moving logs and tells him her name even though her father has told her not to. This shows that their love is really strong.

Ferdinand really loves Miranda because he moves the logs when he wouldn't normally do that because he is a prince, or was one. He thinks she's precious 'precious creature' and doesn't want her to move the logs.

These scenes show that love can make you brave and make you do things you wouldn't normally.

This is level 4 because:

- It focuses on the question and tries to answer it.

- It provides quotations to support ideas but doesn't explain them properly.

- It covers both scenes and clearly knows the play well.

To raise the level the student needs to:

- Make sure the quotations are fully explained; at the moment the 'This shows' part just repeats what has already been said.

- Include some analysis of the language used, including how it makes us respond.
- Include more analysis of the play.

page 182

The language used in these scenes emphasises the high emotions experienced by the characters. Explain how Shakespeare has used the language to create this emotion.

Ariel uses lots of alliteration in his song: 'foot it featly here and there, And sweet sprites bear the burthen.' And 'full fathom five thy father lies'.

Ferdinand personifies the music, 'this music crept by me upon the waters, allaying both their fury and my passion with its sweet air. Thence I have followed it – or it hath drawn me rather.' This makes the water seem to be like a person and that is why it is able to creep and draw him.

Prospero uses horrible language to Miranda: 'wench' which puts her in her place.

Miranda and Ferdinand both say that each other is like a god: 'a thing divine' and 'goddess'. This language shows they think in similar ways and think each other is the same. This is high emotion.

There are lots of exclamation marks. These show high emotion: 'A thousand thousand!' this is the love he feels.

This is level 4 because:

- It shows a general understanding of the characters in these scenes.
- It tries to focus on the question.
- It uses quotations and tries to explain some of them.

To raise the level the student needs to:

- Provide more explanation and analysis of the language used. The quotations should be shorter and the student needs to comment upon specific words and phrases.
- Provide some explanation and analysis of the language techniques used, such as metaphor, simile and alliteration.

pages 184–185

Ferdinand's emotions change dramatically in this play. Imagine you are directing this play. Explain how you want the actor playing Ferdinand to show his thoughts and emotions in these scenes.

When Ferdinand is first speaking he should be half crying because he thinks his father is dead and he is alone on the island and he is scared.

When he sees Miranda his tears should stop and he should stop and look amazed as if she is the most amazing thing he has ever seen. He should hold his hand out and point at her so it is clear what he is talking about. When he says 'O you wonder' he should grab her arm as if he can't help himself.

When he says he is now the king – 'Myself am Naples' – he should be really upset again because he has remembered his father and everyone is dead.

When he says if Miranda is a virgin he will make her the queen he should be happy and excited again to show he loves her.

When he says he isn't a spy he should shake his head to show he isn't.

When he says 'I will resist such entertainment till mine enemy has more power' he should pull out his sword and then freeze as the magic works.

When he follows Prospero out at the end of the scene he should look in love and confused.

In Act 3, scene 1 he should be hot and tired from carrying logs and should look hot and tired.

When Miranda speaks to him he should look happy.

When he asks her name he should look anxious in case she doesn't tell him.

When he finds out her name he should look really happy as she's chosen him over her father and that means she likes him more. He should wave his arms about.

When she says she loves him he should be really happy again.

When they agree to marry he should go on one knee and propose and then kiss her hand.

He is really happy at the end because he is in love and knows Miranda loves him.

This is level 4 because:

- It shows it knows what happens in the scene but focuses on movement and facial expression rather than showing understanding of emotion and the language.

- Some quotations are used but there need to be more.

To raise the level the student needs to:

- Focus the directions on bringing out the meaning of the language.

- Make sure the directions are specific and detailed.

- Try to vary the way paragraphs are started, rather than starting each one with 'When'.

The relationship between Prospero and Miranda is very important. Imagine you are directing this play and explain how you want the actors playing these characters to show their thoughts and emotions in these scenes.

Level 4 (mid)

Prospero has to be really strict all the time and Miranda has to be a bit of a wimp who just falls for the first proper man she sees. Miranda needs to speak in a really high voice to show her amazement at seeing this man who she thinks is like a god, 'a thing divine', this shows she thinks he's like a god so has to look amazed.

Prospero wants her to fall in love with Ferdinand even though he's pretending not to want that, so he needs to rub his hands together with glee when she is talking to Ferdinand and she can't see him (Prospero). This is to show us that he is manipulating them 'it goes on I see as my soul prompts it'. This means what is happening is what he wants to happen.

Miranda needs to show she can't understand why her father is suddenly so horrible to Ferdinand and needs to act surprised.

Prospero needs to be nasty to her to make her think it's real.

By the end of this scene Prospero is acting horribly and Miranda needs to show that she is confused and upset because she thinks Ferdinand is amazing but she doesn't want to disobey her father. We can see that this mattered to her because she doesn't tell Ferdinand her name until into act 3, scene 1 and is then worried about having disobeyed her father, 'O my father, I have broke your hest to say so!' She needs to show she is worried but also her love for Ferdinand is greater than what Prospero

said. As Prospero watches he needs to show he is really happy about what is happening. He doesn't get much to say so the actor needs to show it properly.

This is level 4 because:

- It provides a good understanding of Prospero and Miranda and how they could be portrayed.

- It uses some quotations although these tend just to repeat what has already been stated.

- It covers both scenes and characters.

To raise the level the student needs to:

- Provide a short quotation to go with each idea and try not to repeat the quotation in their own words.

- Be sure to comment about the language and its impact.

- Make sure the directions are specific and detailed.

page 188

Miranda's emotions change dramatically in this play. Imagine you are directing this play and explain how you want the actor playing Miranda to show her thoughts and emotions in these scenes.

Level 4 (high)

When Miranda enters she must show she is really amazed by Ferdinand, 'What is't? A Spirit? Lord, how it looks about! Believe me sir, It carries a brave form. But 'tis a spirit' and then 'I might call him a thing divine, for nothing natural I ever saw so noble'. In these lines she is saying she thinks he is not human but he is a spirit and then she says he's divine which means that he is like a god. When she says these words she has to show she is trying to work out who he is and what he is and so she needs to show that she is amazed and full of wonder. She needs to emphasise the word 'divine' as that is the most important one, as it says what she thinks of him and to think he is a god is pretty impressive.

When Miranda argues with her father she needs to show this is probably the first time she has done so and needs to get more and more certain and get more power into her voice as she realises it is something she can do and he won't strike her down with his magic for doing it. When she says 'O dear father! Make not too rash a trial of him, for He's gentle, and not fearful', she needs to emphasise the contrast of the words 'gentle' and 'fearful' to show they are opposites and also that gentle also means noble and well brought up just like her and not like Caliban.

When she tells Ferdinand she loves him she needs to be a bit worried that he might run off but also secure in her own feelings and certain that she loves him. She should cry at this part.

This is level 4 because:

- It shows really good understanding of Miranda and how she must be feeling.
- It provides some explanation of the language used and how key words are important.
- Quotations are used but they are far too long.

To raise the level the student needs to:

- Use shorter quotations – just the most important bit without repeating an idea over and over again.
- Include more about the meaning of the language.
- Make the answer balanced so there is the same amount on both scenes.

Romeo and Juliet

page 177

1 1C, 2D, 3A, 4B

2

Quotation	Technique	Effect
'the bud bit with an envious worm'	alliteration of 'b'	Reflects the harsh and secret way the worm has infected the bud
'O brawling love, O loving hate'	oxymoron	Makes us really consider the qualities of these emotions – we see they are not as simple as we might assume
'What light through yonder window breaks? It is the east, and Juliet is the sun'	Metaphor – says she is the sun	Gives all the qualities of the sun to Juliet: life-giving, warm, light, overwhelming...
'love's light wings'	alliteration	Links these ideas together and makes them trip off the tongue as if they are light and bouncy
'Love goes toward love as schoolboys from their books'	Simile – love as schoolboys leaving their work	Uses a comparison we can all relate to – how eagerly students leave their studies – this is how eagerly love goes to love

page 179

How does Romeo change in these scenes?

Level 4 (low)

Romeo starts off in love and ends up in love but it's a different sort of love. He ends in real love even though he thought he was in real love to start with, but it wasn't. He changes because he learns what real love is. When he sees Juliet he really knows that she is the one.

In the first extract Romeo is just going on and on about being in love but he's not really. He is just enjoying going on about love and imagining that he is in love. He goes on about the time taking forever and seeming really slow, 'sad hours seem long'. This means he thinks the time goes slowly. He says this because the woman he loves doesn't love him. This makes him say lots of oxymorons like 'O brawling love, O loving hate, O heavy lightness, serious vanity, Misshapen chaos of well-seeming forms, feather of lead, bright smoke, cold fire, sick health, still waking-sleep'. These are all oxymorons.

The way he talks makes it sound like he is enjoying being in love even though the girl won't have him and he tries to confuse Benvolio. This shows he enjoys being rejected in love.

However, when he sees Juliet he changes his mind as she is prettier and like the sun and stars. 'Juliet is the sun'. This means he thinks she is the sun which means that he thinks the world should go round her, like it does for the real sun. This is a metaphor.

This is level 4 because:

- It makes some good points about Romeo, such as him enjoying being rejected in love.

- It gives an overview of the way Romeo behaves in each scene.

- It uses quotations but these are too long and not explained fully.

To raise the level the student needs to:

- Plan the answer so the introduction can give a clear overview without being confusing.

- Use short quotations that provide evidence for the ideas.

- Provide explanation of the impact of the quotations, not just a rephrase.

page 181

How is the theme of love explored in these scenes?

Level 4 (mid)

This play shows that love can make you sad or happy. It can make you do things you wouldn't normally do like mope around in the woods or climb enemy walls.

Romeo is really in love with Rosaline as he calls her 'precious treasure'. This shows us that he thinks she's really valuable and precious like treasure.

Then Romeo falls in love with Juliet and we know this because he says she is the sun, 'It is the east and Juliet is the sun'. This shows us that he thinks she's warm and glowing like the sun and that all the people like all the planets go round her. That's why he's in love with her. He also says she's a bright angel, 'bright angel'. This means he thinks she's like an angel. This shows us he is in love with her.

Juliet is in love with Romeo and asks him to marry her so she must be serious. This shows love can make you do things you wouldn't normally do, like marry someone who is basically a stranger.

This is level 4 because:

- It focuses on the question and tries to answer it.
- It provides quotations to support ideas although it doesn't explain them properly.
- It covers both scenes and clearly knows the play well.

To raise the level the student needs to:

- Make sure the quotations are fully explained; at the moment the 'This shows' part just repeats what has already been said.
- Include some analysis of the language used, including how it makes us respond.
- Include more analysis of the play.

How is the idea of deception explored in these scenes?

Level 4 (mid)

Different people are deceived in this play. Romeo is deceived because he thinks he is in love with Rosaline when he isn't really. It also talks about smoke and night and times when you can't see properly and so are deceived.

Romeo thinks he's in love with Rosaline and goes on about it all the time to Benvolio and is really miserable but he's not really, he's in love with Juliet, or is when he meets her and so that's why he says 'he jests at scars that never felt a wound'. This tells us that he knows the feelings he had for Rosaline were wrong and he was deceived about them.

When he sees Juliet in the second scene it's night and is a time when people are deceived and they've just been to the party so might have been taking drugs which mess up your senses. He calls her 'the sun' which means that he's not deceived about her and she turns night into day.

Juliet liked the fact that night was like a curtain and hid her private thoughts 'counsel' but it was also deceptive as she couldn't see that Romeo was there.

This is level 4 because:

- It focuses on the question and tries to answer it.
- It provides quotations to support ideas but doesn't provide analysis of the language.
- It covers both scenes and clearly knows the play well.

To raise the level the student needs to:

- Make sure the quotations are fully explained with reference to the language used.
- Develop each idea more fully so the idea of deception is fully explored.
- Not write about a film version of the play – you are examined on the written play text.

page 183

Romeo and Juliet both play with language. Explain how Shakespeare uses language to show they are a good match.

Level 4 (low)

Romeo uses lots of oxymorons when he talks to Benvolio: 'brawling love, loving hate, heavy lightness. Serious vanity, misshapen chaos'.

Romeo talks about how 'love is a smoke made with the fumes of sighs'. This means that love can make you sad and stop you seeing reality. This is like Juliet because she admits her love in darkness.

Romeo describes Juliet in really good terms, 'bright angel'. This means he thinks she is amazing and heavenly. This is like the way Juliet describes Romeo: 'dear perfection'.

They both use lots of words to say what they mean. They use the same sort of language and this means they are a good match.

This is level 4 because:

- It shows a general understanding of some of the language in these scenes.

- It tries to focus on the question.

- It uses quotations, but these are not always accurate or explained.

To raise the level the student needs to:

- Provide more explanation and analysis of the language used, including comment on the impact of the language on the reader.

- Provide some explanation and analysis of the impact of the language techniques used.

- Make sure all quotations are accurate.

Romeo's language is used to create his personality. Explain how Shakespeare does this.

Level 4 (mid)

Romeo goes on and on about love so it makes him look like he's obsessed with love. He just moans and groans and this makes him look really pathetic. He thinks he's totally in love and that's all he talks about. He calls it a madness: 'a madness most discreet' and this means he thinks love turns you mad. This makes him look like he knows what he is doing, so maybe he's not gone mad with love but is enjoying the love that he is feeling even though she doesn't love him. This makes him seem like a strange person as he likes being sad.

When he is talking about Juliet he is over the top and uses really over the top descriptions of her like being an angel, 'bright angel', and this shows he sees the best and is happy to tell it as he sees it. It makes him seem really positive and enthusiastic.

He doesn't really listen to Juliet and starts to swear on the moon. This shows he doesn't really listen and just does what he thinks is best and doesn't always think things through.

This is level 4 because:

- It tries to answer the question and keeps focus throughout.

- It provides some quotations to support the answer but needs many more.

- It shows good understanding of Romeo.

To raise the level the student needs to:

- Develop the answer fully, writing more about Romeo's language and personality.

- Provide a short quotation for each idea.

- Provide analysis of the language and its impact for each quotation.

page 185

Romeo's emotions change dramatically in this play. Imagine you are directing this play and explain how you want the actor playing Romeo to show his thoughts and emotions in these scenes.

Level 4 (low)

When Romeo enters he should be crying because he is rejected in love.

When he sees Benvolio he should sigh and drop his head and sigh lots more. When he says 'Is the day so young?' he should sound really depressed and show he's really sad and can't believe time is going so slowly for him.

When he says 'Out of her favour where I am in love' he should be really depressed and sigh lots and drag his feet round the stage.

When he does all the oxymorons he should show more passion and energy as he's getting worked up about the fight and forgets himself for a bit.

When he says 'Love is a smoke made from the fume of sighs' he should be really upset again because he has remembered he is not loved by the woman he loves.

When he says 'Thou canst not teach me to forget' he needs to sound really depressed and upset as he thinks the world might as well end if she doesn't love him.

In Act 2, scene 2 he should be excited and jumpy. He has just met and fallen in love with Juliet and finds out that she loves him too and this is really exciting and good news.

When he says 'it is my lady! It is my love!' he has to be really excited as he sees Juliet and is excited about it.

When he hears Juliet speak he should hide a little bit but then be amazed and really happy as she says she loves him.

When he says he'll change his name he should be really excited with his arms out so she sees him.

When he swears he should be really dramatic.

When he goes he should be full of joy.

This is level 4 because:

- It shows the student knows what happens in the scene but focuses on movement rather than showing understanding of emotion and language.

- Some quotations are used but there need to be more.

To raise the level the student needs to:

- Focus the directions on bringing out the meaning of the language.

- Make sure the directions are specific and detailed.

- Try to vary the way paragraphs are started, rather than starting each one with 'When'.

- Try to structure the answer so paragraphs are more than one sentence long.

This is level 4 because:

- It shows understanding of what happens in these scenes.

- It tries to answer the question throughout the answer.

- It gets better as it goes on, suggesting that it would be better if planned.

To raise the level the student needs to:

- Plan the answer so it gets on with answering the question and doesn't repeat itself.

- Include more quotations to support the ideas.

- Provide some comment and explanation of the language.

page 188

What impression do you get of Romeo in these scenes?

Level 4 (mid)

My impression of Romeo is a man who thinks he's in love but then is in love. He starts by thinking he is in love with Rosaline but then he meets Juliet and falls in love with her and never thinks of Rosaline again. He can't be found in the first scene but then he is and is just moaning about Rosaline and saying he loves her but she doesn't love him and won't because she won't let Cupid hit her with his arrow, 'She'll not be hit with Cupid's arrow'. Which means she won't let herself fall in love. Romeo is really upset about this and goes on and on about how great she is and how he loves her. This gives me the impression that he actually likes this sort of love and being the centre of attention as far as Benvolio is concerned. He doesn't care about Benvolio.

In the second scene he is now is love with Juliet and I don't really believe in that love either as he's only just seen her and so he just fancies her. The impression I get of Romeo in this scene is the same, it's just that the girl is different. He says that the stars are Juliet's eyes and she is like an angel: 'speak again, bright angel'. This makes her seem heavenly. It is a good metaphor.